Praise for
All The Right Reasons

"Kevin Guest reminds us that when we really know our brand, we sometimes turn down great opportunities because they divert us from our true mission in life. His stories are inspiring and come at a time when everyone could use some inspiration."
—**Dr. Jennifer Ashton**, ABC News Chief Medical Correspondent, physician, nutritionist, author, and mother

"*All The Right Reasons* hits all the right notes. Kevin Guest offers the equivalent of a GPS system to navigate the road of life and shows that morality, virtue and excellence are the path to achieving greatness! There are reasons why he's advanced one of the leading companies in the world and he gives you all the right reasons you can advance in your life too!"
—**DeVon Franklin**, New York Times bestselling author and award-winning producer

"Once or twice in a lifetime, a book cuts through the noise and grabs us by the soul. This is one of those rare, principle-centered works that guides us to authentic, lasting success."
—**Denis Waitley**, author of *The Psychology of Winning* and *Seeds of Greatness*

"While many leaders talk about the principles of success, few people live them as diligently as Kevin Guest. In this book, Kevin shares the values, beliefs, and mindsets that underpinning the extraordinary success of the USANA business and offers powerful insights into what drives him as an individual. I would recommend *All The Right Reasons* to anyone looking to live a life of influence and lasting success."
—**Michael McQueen**, Trend forecaster, award-winning speaker and 6-time bestselling author

"*All The Right Reasons* is a powerfully inspiring read. Kevin's 12 Principles will have a solid impact on your thinking and on your life."
—**Tony Jeary**, The RESULTS Guy™

"Kevin demonstrates the principles he has used to build a successful life, balancing family, faith and business along the way. His story will inspire and motivate you to adopt these same concepts for all the right reasons."
—**Chuck Coonradt**, author of *The Game of Work*, and grandfather of gamification

All
The
Right
Reasons

Kevin Guest

All The Right Reasons

12 Timeless Principles for Living a Life in Harmony

Kevin Guest

WITH CRAIG CASE AND JENNIFER BECKSTRAND

Foreword by Collin Raye

All The Right Reasons
12 Timeless Principles for Living a Life in Harmony

To order additional copies visit *amazon.com* or *USANA.com*.

Image page 116 courtesy of Immaculée Ilibagiza LLC,
used with permission.

Designer: Morgan Crockett
Contributors: Amy Haran, Tim Brown,
Cindy Yearley, Sean Derber

ISBN: 978-1-7321636-0-7 (English)
ISBN: 978-1-7321636-6-9 (eBook)

Printed in the United States of America

I would like to dedicate this book first and foremost to my wife, best friend, and eternal companion, Lori. Anything good that has happened in my life over the past 34 years is because of you. I feel like I am the richest man on earth, and it's because of you. You have supported me 100 percent while keeping the home fires burning as I have traveled the globe. We have a very loving and close family because of you. Our children are faithful because of your example. I am close to the Lord because of your willingness to accept me with my faults and never let our marriage fade.

Secondly, to our children and grandchildren: Nathan and Tonya Guest (Myka, Eliza, Sophie), Holli and Ian Guzy (Zara, Mae), Ryan and Jessica Guest (Banksy), Stephani and Jess Bluth (Kleo). My life would be incomplete without you and your love. I feel so blessed to be your dad and popa!

I am also extremely grateful to have brothers and sisters, LaMar, Muriel, Marlene, and Mark, who have always been there for their little brother.

And lastly, to my parents, Francis and Venus Guest, my life-long mentors and two of the finest people I have ever known.

Table of Contents

Foreword

by Collin Raye

How many CEOs do you know whose only goal in life was to play in a rock 'n' roll band? As a young man, Kevin Guest desired one thing above everything else. He wanted to perform his music in a band and become famous doing it. Music was his passion and goal, and he worked hard to make it real. Just when the dream was within his grasp, when he could literally reach out and touch it, he followed a divine prompting

COLLIN RAYE
24 Top 10 Records
16 Number 1 Hits
10 Time CMA & ACM Vocalist Nominee

and gave up his quest. Taking another path, he ended up as the CEO of a highly successful, publicly traded, international company.

But as you'll see in this book, Kevin doesn't care as much about his title as he does about doing good to others, improving lives, and making a difference in the world. Other than music, that's what really gets Kevin excited. He's the perfect CEO for a company like USANA Health Sciences.

Kevin would blush to hear me say these things, but one of the reasons he's such a fine man is because he's so unassuming and humble. I mean it from the bottom of my heart when I say that Kevin is one of the finest men I've ever known.

Kevin plays bass guitar in my band whenever his schedule allows. When he travels with us, we tend to discuss subjects people don't usually talk about on tour—at least not with a group of guys who play country music. We talk about God and purpose and contributing constructively to the world. He once told me that his number-one goal is to make a positive difference in the lives of people. Kevin truly lives what he calls **The Dorothy Principle**, which you will learn about in this book. He values every relationship and is continually seeking to make new connections and nurture existing friendships.

If there is a Christian ideal of how a man is supposed live his life, Kevin is it. I once told him, "Kevin, you're such an inspiration to me and you set such an example." He said, "Well, I think life is a bit of a test, and hopefully, I'm passing." I've never seen Kevin make a selfish decision. He thinks of his family, his friends, and his associates at USANA and always tries to put others first. Kevin doesn't get preachy. The way he lives his life is the loudest sermon he could give. You can feel Kevin's goodness when you're with him, and to me, that's the greatest witness of the kind of man he is.

When I first met Kevin, he was a USANA vice president, and he continued to be promoted because of his strong work ethic, his clear vision, his ingenious ideas, and his fertile mind that's always at work. He comes up with new, interesting ideas and creative ways to grow the business, taking USANA to an unprecedented level of achievement. In this book, Kevin shares the solid principles that guide his life and make him a great husband and father, an incredible CEO, and a valued member of the band—whenever he's able to fit us in.

Kevin's achievements are many. He's started more than one business, filmed Gene Simmons, held the Hope Diamond, and played at the Grand Ole Opry. But you will find out why performing at the Grand Ole Opry was one of his greatest accomplishments and also one of his greatest trials. In this book, Kevin shares many such experiences, while offering lessons we all can apply in our lives.

When Kevin comes on tour with me, he jumps right in to help set up our equipment instead of waiting for others to do the work. He's *The Holland Principle* in action. He brings a positive feeling whenever he plays with the band. Occasionally one of the musicians in the band will say, "That bass player sure is a nice guy." They have no idea what Kevin does when he's not playing music because he's never arrogant or self-important. After Kevin goes home, I tell my band Kevin is the CEO of a billion-dollar company, and they can hardly believe it.

I've called Kevin many times over the years when I had a business or personal issue and needed some guidance. It's one of the reasons I was so excited to hear he was going to write this book—he has tremendous wisdom to share. And for as kind and caring as he is, Kevin also possesses rare strength and quiet authority that encourage people to trust him. He carries his many responsibilities comfortably, like a backpack. I've watched him interact with the USANA employees and Associates all over the world. They love him, and he loves them. He's an exceptional leader and an incredible friend.

People cross paths for a reason, and Kevin's entrance into my life has been nothing but a blessing to me. As you read this book, you'll not only come to appreciate who Kevin is, but you'll learn some of the principles Kevin lives by that make him such a happy, blessed, extraordinary man. I hope you come to love Kevin as I do.

I'd Rather See a Sermon

By Edgar A. Guest

I'd rather see a sermon than hear one any day;
I'd rather one would walk with me than merely tell the way.

The eye's a better pupil, and more willing than the ear,
Fine counsel is confusing, but example's always clear.

The best of all the preachers are men who live their creed,
For to see good put into action, is what everyone needs.

I can soon learn how to do it, if you let me see it done,
I can catch your hands in action, but your tongue too fast may run.

And the lecture you deliver may be very wise and true,
But I'd rather get my lesson by observing what you do.

For I may misunderstand you in the high advice you give,
But there is no misunderstanding how you act and how you live.

When I see an act of kindness, I am eager to be kind;
When a weaker brother stumbles, and a stronger stays behind.
Just to see if I can help him, then the wish grows strong in me,

To be as big and thoughtful as I know that friend to be.
And all travelers can witness that the best of guides today,
Is not the one that tells them, but the one that shows the way.

Introduction

My dad's hands always seemed extra large to me, even as I grew to maturity and he shrunk with age. His were strong hands, hands that had seen work and war and weariness, hands that had wiped away tears and drawn me in for many an embrace. In the waning years before his death, my father's hands looked like a road map of his life. Prominent veins crisscrossed the weathered skin, marking a path of joy and sorrow, loving and living. His long, gnarled fingers could still press the valves on his French horn, grip a hammer, pinch a penny, or make a point that was always worth listening to.

By worldly standards, my father was an ordinary man—so ordinary that he passed out of this life without a parade or a lot of fanfare. But those of us who loved him knew that he got much less praise than he deserved but more, I'm sure, than he wanted.

My dad is one of my heroes.

My parents, Francis and Venus Guest, were part of "The Greatest Generation," the generation that grew up during the Great Depression and fought in World War II. Before my parents married, my dad enlisted in the service and became a merchant marine. He was eventually stationed on some of the oil tankers that refueled ships in the Pacific during the second half of the war. Dad was sent into the heart of a number of horrific and now-famous battles that cost the lives of thousands of sailors.

Dad rarely talked about the war, but his experiences in the Pacific impacted him profoundly. Work on the tankers was grueling and relentless. He was separated from his bride for three years, and he constantly faced the very real possibility of death.

With the specter of death and destruction continually before his eyes, my dad could have let the war make him bitter. After all the horrors he'd seen, he might have hardened like stone or become a shell of the man he had been. Instead, my dad chose to see miracles in the midst of tragedy, and he returned home with a deep conviction that God is real and that He not only guides the stars but the lives of every person on this earth. Dad imbued our family with that same faith.

In our home, we prayed and studied the scriptures. We went to church every Sunday and regularly talked of God's goodness, mercy, and grace. We learned we are all God's children and He wants us to love and serve each other. My parents instilled me with a deep faith in a higher power. My faith in God is my anchor, my solid foundation in any storm. I would be nothing without it.

In the ways that really count, my parents were truly extraordinary. They lived their lives serving and teaching others, not the least of whom were their children. Virtue meant something to my mom and dad, and threads of kindness, hard work, and integrity wove the strong cords of character in their lives. My parents' lessons, both spoken and lived, shaped the man I have become and the person I still hope to be. *All the Right Reasons* is, in part, a tribute to them.

WHAT KIND OF PERSON DRIVES AWAY?

I often wonder what my dad would think of our world today. News of corrupt politicians, mass shootings, rampant crime, and disintegrating families dominates the airwaves. Would my dad doubt the strength of our character? Would he conclude we've lost our way?

I have recently heard three all-too-common stories that would have troubled my parents.

Haley was stuck in rush hour traffic. She tapped a frustrated rhythm on her steering wheel as the cars in front of her crawled down the freeway. With a terrifying jolt, a truck crashed into the car behind Haley, propelling that car into Haley's car, denting her bumper. Fortunately, Haley wasn't badly hurt. She and the driver behind her pulled to the shoulder, but the truck driver, the one who had caused the accident, sped away. After the shock of the accident wore off, Haley was left to wonder, "What kind of person drives away?"

My friend's elderly father recently got a call from someone pretending to be his grandson who said he needed money because he was in trouble with the police in Mexico. My friend's father knew the call was a scam, but it made him ask, "What kind of person preys on another's worst fears for money?"

A star player on a college basketball team got suspended for breaking team rules. Unfortunately, his suspension came at the end of the season when his team was trying to make the playoffs. Because he was suspended, the player's team lost a pivotal game. Fans and teammates alike couldn't understand. "Why would someone let down his team for momentary pleasure?"

I don't know the answers to these questions, but I do know that if our choices aren't built on a solid foundation of worthy values, our lives and livelihoods, relationships and reputations will crumble, and we will be left to wonder what went wrong.

Life is full of choices. One study suggests we make up to 35,000 decisions a day.[1] Each choice, mundane or pivotal, has consequences we don't often anticipate or comprehend. Over time and almost imperceptibly, our decisions are woven together like threads in a blanket. These threads make up the quality of our lives and the nature of our characters.

Boyd Matheson, a friend of mine and former chief of staff to U.S. Senator Mike Lee, said, "Integrity and morality are core character traits. Such traits form the basis of personal strength and are the driving forces that enable individuals to do what is right—under pressure or when no one is looking."[2]

Character traits such as trustworthiness, kindness, and loyalty can fortify companies, marriages, friendships, and families. My parents understood that the lack of such values can shake the very foundations of every career we pursue, every project we undertake, and every relationship we cherish.

Thread by thread, choice by choice, we weave a character.

A LIFE IN HARMONY

Putting our core character traits into action is what it means to *live a life in harmony.*

In music, harmony occurs when notes blend in a way that is pleasing to the ear. Whether someone plays in a band, sings in a choir, or performs in an orchestra, there is nothing quite as exhilarating as achieving perfect harmony with fellow musicians. Harmony in music doesn't happen without hours of practice and each individual musician's commitment to getting the music right.

A life in harmony means a consistent and honest arrangement of your values and a solid commitment to living those values day in and day out.

When I was young, I lived music down to my bones, and harmonies played constantly in my head. I wanted to be a rock star more than anything else. But life took me in a different direction, and I've learned a different kind of harmony. For the past three decades, I have been a leader at USANA Health Sciences, one of the finest nutritional supplement and direct sales companies in the world. My life experiences have far exceeded any expectations I had in my youth.

We all have defining moments in our lives—times when our choices align with our destiny and catapult us in an unanticipated direction. These moments can paralyze or break us, leave us gasping for air or wondering what went wrong. Or they can transform us, profoundly reshaping us for the better, leaving us with fresh insights, new goals, and strengthened resolve. More than once, I have stood at a crossroads, sometimes understanding the far-reaching consequences of my decisions, other times oblivious that something important was about to happen. My success has been, in great part, because I try to remain true to the values my parents taught me. While I have done many things right, I have also made my share of mistakes and learned some of life's most important lessons the hard way.

Even if some of my choices turned out to be wrong, I can truly say I made each choice for all the right reasons. And in the end, the reasons are what matter most.

It could be easy to feel helpless reading headlines about corrupt politicians, divisiveness on social media, or rampant dishonesty. My parents faced their generation's own unique, sometimes horrific, challenges with bravery, sacrifice, and love. They tried to live their lives in harmony with what they knew to be true. Each of us has a similar choice: to meet problems with solutions, to fight corruption with integrity, to answer callousness with kindness.

In this book, I share twelve principles I have done my best to live by. I also share the reasons behind these principles. I hope these reasons and principles will help you build your own solid foundation and help you create a life in harmony.

This book is a message of hope, a plea for courage, and a clarion call to action. Who will have character if you don't? Who will fight for virtue, stand for integrity, and love truth? Who will right the wrongs, heal the wounds, and repair the broken, if not you?

Will you join me in this quest for character?

Will you seek harmony?

Will you live your life for all the right reasons?

Why should we build on a solid foundation?

Because Storms Will Rage

My parents owned a sawmill.

For several years, my dad was a bookkeeper for Superior Buildings Lumber Company, a small lumber mill in the Flathead Valley of northwestern Montana. The owner was so fond of my dad, he gave him a small percentage of the business as a gift. After the owner died, his family sold the lumber mill to my parents and a partner.

My parents took an enormous risk purchasing the lumber mill. They mortgaged their house as collateral, leveraging their life savings to secure the loan. They depended on the success of the mill to make the payments on the loan.

Late one afternoon, one of my dad's trusted employees started a fire while he was welding, and the sawmill burned to the ground. My parents were devastated, but because kindness and forgiveness were two of my dad's core values, I don't remember ever hearing him say anything derogatory about that employee. In fact, that employee continued to work at the mill for many years.

Instead of wallowing in their misfortunes, my dad and his partner immediately started rebuilding, utilizing their existing inventory and putting as many employees as possible to work. They built a new mill, bigger and better than the one they'd lost.

My dad had nurtured many business relationships over the years, and he had a reputation for being a man of principle. Because they trusted deeply in my dad's integrity, bankers, customers, and suppliers all came to his aid during a very difficult time.

I CAN SLEEP THROUGH A STORM

An unknown author told the story of a young man who applied for a job as a farmhand. When the farmer asked about his qualifications, he said, "I can sleep through a storm." The farmer wasn't quite sure what he meant, but he hired the young man anyway. Several weeks later, a severe storm blew through the farm. The farmer jumped out of bed calling for his farmhand, but the young man was sound asleep. The farmer quickly ran outside to tie down his wheat, only to find it had already been bound and covered. The shutters had been securely fastened, and the animals were safely in the barn and provided with plenty of feed. There was even a tall stack of logs next to the fireplace. The farmer finally understood the young man's words: Because he was prepared for the storm, he could sleep in peace.

Sometimes things happen at USANA that test the company and me to the core. As the company expands internationally, it seems that issues arise with increasing frequency. Most aren't Category 5 hurricanes, but all have the potential to make us lose our bearings and knock us off course.

A few years ago, we discovered microbes in one of our products during our quality control process. We had a decision to make: We could use a process to kill the microbes and sell the product, sell the product with the microbes, or scrap the entire lot. This was a multimillion-dollar decision. If we had sold the products as they were, almost certainly no one would have known. Even though microbes can cause disease, the chances of any negative reactions were almost zero.

But as a team, there really wasn't any need for a discussion. Product quality is a critical differentiator for USANA, an area where we refuse to compromise, so we scrapped the entire lot and discontinued the product offering until a complete solution could be identified.

On another occasion, a person who stood to gain greatly from a drop in our stock price published a report on USANA, making numerous false accusations. We received calls from concerned distributors, tense regulators, and anxious shareholders. The accusations seriously hurt our image. We could have allowed this person to distract us from our purpose as a company, but the management team made a conscious decision to focus on building the business, executing our business plan, and supporting our employees and distributors. The accuser later ended up in prison due to false claims he'd made against other companies.

I've heard numerous sales pitches for cheaper products that would increase our profit margins. "The products don't have to be better than good enough," I've been told. "At a certain point, you're throwing away money." These arguments don't impress me. As a company, we have always made a commitment to quality as our highest priority, before cost concerns, before expense, and certainly before popular trends.

I understand and respect the foundation upon which our company was built, just as I am sure of the principles that govern my life. Decisions are always clear when we stick to our values and principles. Our company mettle has been tested through many storms. Today, USANA is a stronger company because we stay focused on our mission and make the right choices for the right reasons.

In some ways, being a CEO is like captaining a ship. There are violent storms and mammoth waves, tranquil seas and brilliant sunsets. I have learned to love the waves and the winds as much as I love the calm water and spectacular horizons. Storms and adversity test our strength, keep us vigilant, and propel us forward. And much like the farmhand in the story, if we build our lives on a foundation of solid values, we have nothing to fear.

One of my primary responsibilities as CEO is to plan for the future and make ideas come to life. Successful leaders are the ones with the vision and courage to take a concept from paper to reality. Making ideas come alive involves envisioning solutions, navigating roadblocks, weathering conflict and controversy, and solving complex and frustrating problems.

All managers and employees are called upon to solve problems. How those problems are solved is where values, integrity, and a sure foundation make the difference. Problems can be addressed in many ways. A certain fix may require additional resources and produce fewer results in the short term but is the right thing to do. Another answer might be easier, less public, but laced with ethical dilemmas that will hurt the company in the long run. During these times when the pressure to do the expedient thing is high and the patience required to do the right thing is low, a solid foundation is essential.

WHAT IS A SOLID FOUNDATION?

The foolish man built his house on the sand, "and the rain descended, and the floods came, and the winds blew, and beat upon that house; and it fell: and great was the fall of it."[3]

The wise man built his house on a rock "and the rain descended, and the floods came, and the winds blew, and beat upon that house; and it fell not: for it was founded upon a rock."[4]

You build your life on a solid foundation when you define what values are most important to you and make a commitment to live by those values. A solid foundation is personal moral excellence— your awareness of right and wrong, your understanding that there will always be hard decisions, and your commitment to do the right thing—no matter the consequences.

I have always had three priorities on which I've built my life: My first priority is God, second is my family, and third is my career. These are my core principles, and every decision I make is based on this sure foundation.

You stand on solid ground when you recognize the right decision and do the right thing for the right reasons, even if it's going to take longer, be more expensive, cause you inconvenience, make you unpopular, or leave you standing all alone.

When I was a young father, playing with my band often required me to perform on Saturday nights, and sometimes I'd get home at 3:00 a.m. or even later on Sunday morning. I had promised myself that I would never miss going to church, even if I was out late the night before, and I kept that promise. My children saw how important my faith was to me. I didn't just profess my belief—I lived it.

Because of my position at USANA, there have been times in my extensive overseas travel when my flight has arrived in Salt Lake City on Sunday morning and I have gone home, put on a suit, and headed straight to my church meetings. It would be easy to justify missing church to catch up on my sleep, but I have built my life on certain foundational principles that I won't compromise, even for a little rest. If I feel myself nodding off at church, I hold my feet a few inches off the ground. It increases blood flow and helps me stay awake. If anyone notices my strange behavior, they're kind enough not to mention it.

Even though my band played in a lot of bars when I was younger, I've never taken a drink of alcohol or tried illegal drugs. I always wanted to be true to my values, and I've never felt I had to compromise my principles to achieve my goals and live life to the fullest. I'm pretty sure I'm the only Mormon bishop who has ever been on stage with Ozzy Osbourne.

I'm not saying I'm perfect. I have made many mistakes of which I am not proud, but I try to learn from those mistakes and never repeat them.

During one production I was involved in, I was surrounded by people who regularly used foul language. This language bothered me because I was taught that what we say is an outward sign of our inner values. The words we use can have a great impact on the people around us; they can build or tear down, lift or offend. I pulled out a jar and told my fellow workers it was the "Cuss Jar." Whenever they said a bad word, they were required to put a coin in the jar. My friends laughed but good-naturedly agreed to put money in the jar every time they said a bad word. For a few days, the language didn't change much, and the jar filled up quickly. The whole group went out to dinner with the money from the jar. But eventually, the Cuss

Jar made my friends more aware of the words they were using, and the foul language problem improved. Twenty-five years later, those friends still laugh about the Cuss Jar.

A PERSONAL COMMITMENT TO A SOLID FOUNDATION

I believe in order to succeed in today's extreme business environment, a commitment to a solid foundation is vital. The pressure for profits, power, and personal aggrandizement is as unrelenting as the problems they produce. This is why it is so important for people to know what they stand for and to commit to living according to those values.

Benjamin Franklin, philosopher and one of America's founding fathers, was ten years old when he apprenticed to his older brother to learn the trade of printing, an occupation he was proud to claim throughout his distinguished life. In 1726, at the age of twenty, Franklin made a commitment to live according to his "moral virtues." In his autobiography, he explained how he set about to achieve what he called, "moral perfection."

> It was about this time I conceived the bold and arduous project of arriving at moral perfection. I wished to live without committing any fault at any time; I would conquer all that either natural inclination, custom, or company might lead me into.[5]

He resolved to go about "always doing right, and to avoid any wrongdoing." In order to accomplish this lofty goal, Franklin identified twelve virtues around which to align his life. He wrote a short statement clarifying the meaning of each virtue. Upon completion, he proudly showed his list to a friend, who counseled him to add *humility* to the list.[6]

Franklin's thirteen virtues are:

1   *Temperance.* Eat not to dullness; drink not to elevation.

2   *Silence.* Speak not but what may benefit others or yourself; avoid trifling conversation.

3   *Order.* Let all your things have their places; let each part of your business have its time.

4   *Resolution.* Resolve to perform what you ought; perform without fail what you resolve.

5   *Frugality.* Make no expense but to do good to others or yourself; i.e., waste nothing.

6   *Industry.* Lose no time; be always employ'd in something useful; cut off all unnecessary actions.

7   *Sincerity.* Use no hurtful deceit; think innocently and justly, and, if you speak, speak accordingly.

8   *Justice.* Wrong none by doing injuries, or omitting the benefits that are your duty.

9   *Moderation.* Avoid extremes; forbear resenting injuries so much as you think they deserve.

10 *Cleanliness.* Tolerate no uncleanliness in body, cloaths [sic], or habitation.

11 *Tranquility.* Be not disturbed at trifles, or at accidents common or unavoidable.

12 *Chastity.* Rarely use venery but for health or offspring, never to dullness, weakness, or the injury of your own or another's peace or reputation.

13 *Humility.* Imitate Jesus and Socrates.

Initially, Franklin tried to perfect all of the virtues in himself at once but found the task overwhelming. He decided to concentrate on one virtue for a week at a time, while still tracking his progress in all other areas. He did so by recording his progress at the end of each day, giving himself a black mark for any virtues in which he'd strayed. Franklin could cycle through each virtue four times a year—keeping his values fresh in his mind. At the age of seventy-nine, Franklin wrote that he hadn't yet achieved perfection, but he had discovered something else:

> Tho' I never arrived at the perfection I had been so ambitious of obtaining, but fell far short of it, yet I was, by the endeavor [sic], a better and a happier man than I otherwise should have been if I had not attempted it.[7]

By writing, prioritizing, tracking, and clarifying his core values, Franklin not only understood them better, but he developed a path for integrating them into his life.

In addition to his lifelong career as a printer, Franklin was an author, a political theorist, a scientist, a musician, an inventor, and a politician. He is also the only person whose signature is on four of the most important founding documents of the United States: the Declaration of Independence, the Treaty of Paris, the Treaty of Alliance with France, and the U.S. Constitution. Ben Franklin is revered as one of the most prodigious, practical, and influential men ever to have lived.

TEMPERANCE.						
EAT NOT TO DULNESS; DRINK NOT TO ELEVATION.						
	S.	M.	T.	W.	T.	F.	S.
T.							
S.	•	•		•		•	
O.	• •	•	•		•	•	•
R.			•			•	
F.		•			•		
I.			•				
S.							
J.							
M.							
C.							
T.							
C.							
H.							

Ben Franklin's quest for improvement and his commitment to his core values are what I call **The Ben Franklin Principle:** *When you commit to living your core values, you change your destiny.*

You will know you are succeeding, not only because of how you feel, but also because of the way people respond to you. When you build on a solid foundation and truly live your core values, your friends, family, and co-workers will come to trust and rely on you. They will consult you for advice, seek your guidance, and want to be around you because you inspire them to be better people. They will know you are a person who strives for excellence, a person they can trust to make the right choices for yourself and your company.

When we build a solid foundation on core values and align those core values with our actions, we take charge of our own destinies, have more fulfilling relationships, and achieve long-term, genuine harmony and happiness in business and life.

THE BEN FRANKLIN PRINCIPLE

*When you commit to living according to
your core values, you change your destiny.*

Why did my dad take my mom to the store on his bike?

Because My Parents Were Willing to Sacrifice For What Was Important to Them

My parents bought a piano before they bought a car. When my dad returned from the war after being away for almost three years, the first thing my parents bought was a piano. In those early days without a car, my dad rode his bike to work and took my mom on the back of his bicycle on trips to the store. Some people couldn't understand it. My parents didn't have a car, but they had a beautiful piano. Music was that important to them—essential, actually. My family still owns that piano, by the way.

My parents loved music, and it seemed we were always singing, playing, or listening to records or the radio. My dad was an exceptional musician. As a teenager, he played the French horn in the Twin Falls, Idaho City Band, and later he played in the Kalispell, Montana Community Orchestra. A few years before he died, Dad had that same French horn refurbished so he could keep playing it. He loved that horn. He also had a beautiful tenor voice and was often asked to sing at funerals, church meetings, and musical events. Mom regularly accompanied him on the piano.

For many a Christmas and birthday, I received musical gifts from my parents. The first gift I remember was a cheap little drum set purchased from the Sears catalog. Every Christmas I'd receive an instrument that was a little bit better, a little higher quality.

My dream as a kid was to become a rock star, to play my music for adoring fans, maybe even to be heard on the radio. I played basketball and enjoyed sports like many of my friends, but creating, composing, and performing music was my passion at a very early age. I daydreamed for hours, imagining myself on stage in front of tens of thousands of screaming admirers who loved my music. That dream was a driving force in my life.

We all have dreams. Some dreams are big and fanciful, like being in a movie. Some dreams are sensible, like having a secure retirement. All dreams take work—quite honestly, more work than most people are willing to shoulder.

How many people would buy a piano before they bought a car? Only those with a dream so big, they're willing to pedal to the store instead of drive.

My parents taught me **The Piano Principle**: *When you really want something, make it happen.*

Mom and Dad didn't just sit around wishing there was music in their home. They spent their limited resources on what was most important to them. If you want something badly enough, you give up your time, money, and energy. You roll up your sleeves and get to work. You make the sacrifices necessary to make your dreams come true.

THE ART OF MOWING LAWNS

When I was a young teenager, I decided I needed a professional-grade drum set in order to make my dreams come true. The drum set I wanted was too expensive for my parents. My dad agreed to co-sign on a loan with me if I agreed to do whatever work was necessary to make the monthly payments. The manager at the bank told me he didn't normally make such loans to boys my age, but because of his great relationship with my dad, he gave me the loan. I got a payment book of coupons with the monthly payment amount and due date listed on each coupon.

At the time I got the loan, my band didn't have any paying gigs, and I needed a more dependable source of income. I came up with the idea to mow lawns to make my loan payments. It was harder than I expected to find lawns to mow, but I finally landed a job mowing an entire baseball field.

You know how big a baseball field is? Well, it seems even bigger when you have to mow it with a push mower, which was all our family owned. My mom drove me and the lawn mower to the field each week. I divided the job into sections so it didn't seem so overwhelming—first mowing the infield, then the outfield. I spent hours mowing that field, straining up and down the grass with my push mower, concentrating on keeping straight lines and dreaming of the music I could make with my new drum set. The money I earned mowing that summer was enough to make the payments on my drums. Thanks to that baseball field, I was able to keep my part of the agreement.

In high school, I played the drums and other percussion instruments, but in college, there were a lot of talented drummers, many better than I was. In order to keep earning money with my music, I decided to become a bass guitar player. Because of the complexity of playing the bass, many bass guitarists don't sing and play at the same time, but I could do both. This skill was a real asset. I always had work.

My ability to play and sing together didn't come easily. The skill took hours of practice and an unwavering commitment to my goals, but because I knew *The Piano Principle*, I didn't give up.

Even now, if I could do any one thing, I would play in a band with people who love to make music as much as I do. When the music comes from the heart, the connection between musician and audience is exhilarating and stunningly honest. Music speaks to the soul like nothing else can. This love for music, this awe I have for the process, has been with for me as long as I can remember. Music has transformed my life.

I consider myself an average musician, but I do have a talent for music—mostly because music was always in my home and I learned to love it. But raw talent will only get you so far. At some point, you need to couple your talent with work and a great deal of practice. Only after countless dedicated hours of hard work will natural talent shine.

MICHAEL JORDAN WAS ALWAYS THE LAST TO LEAVE

Steve Alford, former NBA player and current coach of the UCLA Bruins, was only a sophomore in college when he played on the 1984 Olympic gold medal basketball team with Michael Jordan, Patrick Ewing, and other NBA stars. Being able to play with some of the best basketball players in the world was one of the most incredible experiences of his life. Alford said, "When I played with Michael Jordan on the Olympics team, there was a huge gap between his ability and the ability of the other great players on that team. But what impressed me was that he was always the first one on the floor and the last one to leave."[8] Alford recognized *The Piano Principle* in Michael Jordan. Regardless of his natural talent, Michael Jordan became the great player he was, in part, because he put in the time to become great. Even at his peak, he worked harder than most anyone.

There's a lot to be said for effort and sacrifice. I believe they are key components of success in any endeavor.

Swimmer Michael Phelps is the most decorated athlete. He finished his Olympic career with twenty-three gold medals and twenty-eight overall. No one else in Olympic history has even come close to such an accomplishment. Phelps has tremendous natural talent and the physical attributes ideal for a swimmer, but these aren't the only, or even the main reasons he won so many medals. Phelps had a relentless commitment to doing whatever was required to achieve his goals. He trained for over twelve years, putting in thousands of hours in what he describes as "horrible, horrible workouts," swimming 10,000 meters as fast as he could. Each 10,000-meter swim took him two and a half hours. For one five-year stretch, he didn't miss a single day of practice, even on Christmas. Phelps said he worked so hard because he wanted to do something no one had ever done before. "That's what got me out of bed every day. You can't put a limit on anything. The more you dream, the farther you get."[9] Phelps coupled his dreams with focused discipline and an unyielding commitment to hard work. It was this combination that brought about his phenomenal success.

THE SAME SONGS OVER AND OVER AGAIN

My band in junior high and high school succeeded, in part, because of the many hours we spent practicing. We were all good musicians individually, but we had to learn to play together. For some of us, working together didn't come naturally. It took hours of practice in my parents' basement playing the same songs over and over again before we got it right. We had passion for music, and we shared a vision of what we could become. But unless we spent the time, our vision had no chance of becoming a reality.

In *Outliers: The Story of Success*, Malcolm Gladwell proposes that one of the most important reasons the Beatles achieved their extraordinary success was because of the incredible amount of time they spent playing together before they made it big.

> The Beatles ended up traveling to Hamburg five times between 1960 and the end of 1962. On the first trip, they played 106 nights of five or more hours a night. Their second trip they played 92 times. Their third trip they played 48 times, for a total of 172 hours on stage. The last two Hamburg stints, in November and December 1962, involved another 90 hours of performing. All told, they performed for 270 nights in just over a year and a half. By the time they had their first burst of success in 1964, they had performed live an estimated 1,200 times, which is extraordinary. Most bands today don't perform 1,200 times in their entire careers. The Hamburg crucible is one of the things that set the Beatles apart.[10]

In her profound book, *Grit: The Power of Passion and Perseverance,* psychology professor Angela Duckworth makes the case that extraordinary success is a combination of passion and perseverance, in her words, "grit." Dr. Duckworth defines grit as one's "sustained, enduring devotion" to a singularly important goal over a long period of time, regardless of what gets in the way. Duckworth believes grit is the common hallmark of high achievers, from spelling bee champions to Chess Grand Masters to Navy SEALs. She says grit is far more important to achievement than natural talent and is a better predictor of success than virtually any other quality or measurement.[11] Even though Michael Jordan and Michael Phelps have innate talent, their achievements are a result of their unrelenting hard work and perseverance.

Duckworth found scientific evidence that grit, like playing the piano or shooting free throws, can be learned, developed, and enhanced. We don't have to sit around and wish we had it.[12]

PLAYING WITH A SUPERSTAR

The Piano Principle and years of "grit" gave me an opportunity I never could have dreamed of. A few years ago, we needed some quality entertainment for a USANA annual convention. On a whim, I reached out to Collin Raye's manager, Pat Melfi. Collin Raye is one of the greatest country music singers of our time and one of my musical heroes. I love his style, his core values, and his music.

In the 1990s, Collin Raye had twenty-four top-ten records and sixteen number-one hits. He was also a ten-time Male Vocalist of the Year nominee. At the Country Radio Seminar in 2001, Clint Black presented Collin with the organization's Humanitarian of the Year award in recognition of his issue-oriented music and his tireless charity work.

I had never met Collin when I reached out to Pat Melfi to see if Collin would be the mainstage entertainment at the USANA convention. I told Pat I had a band, The Free Radicals—made up mostly of USANA employees—that was exceptionally good and asked if Collin would consider performing with my band instead of bringing his own. Pat agreed to bring Collin to a rehearsal to audition our band. Collin loved our band and agreed to let us play with him at the convention. That night, Collin discovered my passion for music. After the show, he and I became very close friends.

Collin liked the way I played, and he unexpectedly invited me to tour with his band. I was astonished, thrilled, and terrified all at the same time. With the encouragement of Dave Wentz, my boss at USANA, I accepted Collin's invitation. Since I was working full-time at USANA as an officer of the company, the understanding was that my touring with him would be temporary.

I traveled and performed with the band whenever I was available. I would fly from Salt Lake and meet the tour bus. At every performance, about ten minutes before the band went on stage, Collin would make a list of songs we were going to play. Every band member was expected to know his catalogue of songs. Most of Collin's band members had been playing with him for years, so they had mastered all of Collin's music. But, for me, learning and memorizing dozens of songs was a monumental task.

I spent hours at home learning the music and honing my skills. Although I love music and love to play, it was hard work. After working a full day at USANA, instead of relaxing and watching television, I learned how to play every one of Collin Raye's songs. I honestly wondered if I had bitten off more than I could chew. I was only able to persevere with the support of my wife, Dave Wentz, and my own inner voice urging me to endure.

It would have been so easy to quit. I could have called Collin and explained I wasn't ready, and I'm certain he would have understood. Instead, I kept practicing and practicing. If my dad could pedal my mom to the store on a bicycle, I could practice my guitar.

The first time I played with the band, there was no rehearsal beforehand. We were in Florida at the grand opening of a large club, and our performance was broadcast on the radio. I was more than a little intimidated, but my preparation and grit saw me through. I was so grateful I played well and didn't let my bandmates down. Collin was pleased.

Touring with Collin Raye and his band is always a remarkable experience. I work my heart out to make sure my performance is flawless, because it's Collin's career and his product I'm presenting. When Collin has new material, he sends it to me and I learn it so I'm always ready to play. Working with Collin has allowed me to play with and meet some of the finest musical talent on the planet in some of the most famous settings in the music world. I've performed with Collin Raye when we shared the stage with Brooks and Dunn, Keith Urban, Diamond Rio, and many others. It's also been my privilege to play at the Grand Ole Opry in Nashville.

Being gritty has made all the difference.

So much of life comes down to understanding your passion and having the willingness and grit to turn it into something great. It's easy to dream. It's not difficult to discover what you're good at. The hard part is doing the work. The hard part is developing the grit. The hard part is *The Piano Principle.*

THE PIANO PRINCIPLE

When you really want something, make it happen.

Why did I have to overcome my fears?

Because Gene Simmons Wasn't Going to Wait for Me to Learn How to Run a Camera

I loved hanging out with my grandpa Garlan Decatur Qualls. For many years, I was practically his shadow. He was gregarious, outgoing, and had a great sense of humor. He'd take me to the fair or Glacier Park, and we'd sit on a bench, watch the people who walked by, and talk and laugh. I loved being with him.

Grandpa owned a light blue Ford Thunderbird he loved with all his heart. He took offense if anyone passed him on the road, and he would stomp on his gas pedal and turn the affront into a race. Grandpa often left other cars in his dust.

People in town would stop him on the street and ask about something he was selling or some business deal he had going. He loved to make things happen, not only in business, but in life. He was full of enthusiasm and optimism, a real dealmaker. His favorite mottos were written on a plaque that sat on his desk: *You Gotta Fake It Till You Make It* and *Go, Baby, Go*.

These sayings have stuck with me over the years. Sometimes in life, the first step toward success is acting like you know what you're doing—Fake It Till You Make It. Once you've made that initial leap, then Go, Baby, Go means giving it all you've got for as long as you can. I often think about my grandpa and apply his wisdom in business and in my personal life, but I'm not near as wild a driver as he was.

When I started college, my friend Kelly Thayer owned a video production company that shot videos for weddings. At the time, video was a cutting-edge, high-tech business. Although I had been involved in audio production in high school, the idea of creating videos captivated me. It didn't take long for us to come up with several ideas to expand the business. One of our ideas was to create marketing videos for companies, a novel concept back then. Kelly liked the idea of us working together, and we agreed that I would earn a commission and have the opportunity to work on any deal I arranged. This is how I learned the video production business. I brought in several clients and, a short time later, decided to start my own company with my friend Gil Howe.

BOB HOPE AND A GOLF TOURNAMENT

While completing a college internship at Brigham Young University (BYU), I had the opportunity to organize a golf tournament for the American Indian Services, a BYU service organization. Because it was part of my internship, I was expected to arrange the tournament without getting paid for my time. Although I desperately needed paying jobs, I agreed to the time-consuming role of managing the tournament. I had never organized an event like that before, and I knew it would be a good experience. This was one of those times when I definitely had to fake it till I made it.

Later, when I learned more about the guest list, I was incredibly grateful I had agreed to take the project. Former U.S. President Gerald Ford, who was deeply involved with American Indian Services, attended the event along with comedian Bob Hope and golfing great Johnny Miller.

My classmates and I used our own meager resources to rent quality equipment and spent hours editing the project, but the experience was worth every penny and hour it took. The opportunity to work with highly respected politicians, celebrities, and sports figures opened the door for many future corporate events and projects that otherwise wouldn't have happened. I made contacts and friends who promoted my business for years to come.

Little did I know how foundational that Fake It Till You Make It experience would be for my career. That golf tournament connected me to Dr. Myron Wentz, the founder of USANA, and formed a cornerstone of trust between us.

Also as a result of that one volunteer project, I had the privilege of working with Bob Hope again and began a business relationship with Alan Osmond. When I was a kid, I watched *The Donny and Marie Show* every week. I had dreamed about performing with the Osmonds on the show. Because Gil Howe, my production business partner, had previously worked for the Osmonds, I was asked to be a production manager for Alan and met several Hollywood stars.

During one show, we worked with Mr. T, and I remember thinking my dreams as a kid were really coming true.

Upon graduation from college, I accepted a job in Phoenix and ended my partnership in the production business. Shortly before I got the Arizona job, my wife, Lori, and I bought a car. Lori had grown up in Arizona and tried to talk me into getting a car with air conditioning, but being a kid from Montana, I didn't see the need. One day after we'd moved to the Arizona heat, I accidentally left my watch in the car. The face of the watch melted, and I promised myself I would never discount my wife's opinion again.

Other jobs followed that took our family around the West. We ended up back in Utah where I started another production company with the help of Bob Derber, a friend I met during my employment in California. Although I had a lot of big ideas, our operation was very small. By this time, Lori and I had three kids, and we did everything possible just to keep the business going. Lori kept the books in a small accounting booklet at the kitchen table. I played the guitar in bars on weekends to pay the bills, and I rented or borrowed a camera and editing equipment for every project I took on. At the time, my lack of equipment wasn't much of a roadblock because I had very few projects to work on anyway. Those were lean years, but I didn't feel discouraged. I had a vision of what I wanted to accomplish, and that vision sustained me.

FAKING IT WITH AN $80,000 CAMERA

During my teenage years, KISS was one of the biggest rock bands in the world, in part because of the crazy stunts they performed on stage. The band members were well known for their outrageously painted faces and outlandish costumes. They rose to prominence in the mid-to-late 70s with their elaborate and unique live performances. They breathed fire and spit blood, shot rockets, set fire to the stage, and played smoking guitars—crazy stuff. And I loved it.

Much to my mother's irritation and bewilderment, I hung KISS posters all over my bedroom walls. I frequently listened to their songs and worked hard to learn their music. My band played their songs at dances—songs like *Rock and Roll All Nite*, *Beth*, *Detroit Rock City*, and *King of the Night Time World.* Gene Simmons, one of the founders of KISS, was truly one of my idols.

When I was in eighth grade, my mom took me to my first rock concert. KISS performed, and I couldn't have been more thrilled. During the concert, Mom planted herself safely in the stands while I went down on the floor to get closer to the stage. Little did I know that years later I would actually meet members of the band. My mom must have been shocked to see the band's theatrics, but she didn't complain and later had a good laugh about the experience. My conservative, straight-laced mom attended a KISS concert because she knew it would make her son happy.

When I started my new production company, MTV was just becoming popular, and I still had visions of being a rock star. Because of this passion, I came up with the idea of producing a behind-the-scenes look at the lives of famous rock musicians. My team and I called it *Turn Up The Volume!* and envisioned that the series would tell everything a die-hard fan would want to know about a star's life, including the stories that hadn't been told—what it was like when they were on the road or backstage before a big concert, their inspiration for writing music, and how they put an album together. Those were the kinds of stories I wanted to hear, the ones I knew other fans would be interested in as well. The plan was to sell the videos through music stores. When someone went in to buy a record, our videos would also be available for sale.

I put together a business plan and pitched the idea to an investor. He liked what he heard. A few weeks later, I had enough money to get started. I partnered with rock 'n' roll journalist and publicist, Charrie Foglio who knew almost everyone we needed to know to make the venture successful.

Charrie called late one evening and practically screamed into the phone. "KISS is on tour, and I've set up an interview for us with Gene Simmons! You have to be out there in *two days*." After picking myself up off the floor, I almost swallowed my tongue. Up until that moment, the business hadn't been much more than a good idea. The thought of filming this rock 'n' roll icon was almost more than I could comprehend. I was both thrilled and terrified.

In addition to my utter shock that we were going to interview Gene Simmons, I had a larger issue with the equipment. At the time, the kind of video camera necessary for such an interview cost about eighty thousand dollars. Even renting one for a few days was far more than I could afford. Our business was a start-up, and before we'd produced anything, I was scheduled to interview one of the biggest rock stars in the world. It was time to pull out my grandpa's advice: Fake It Till You Make It.

Early the next morning, I visited a local video equipment dealer, who happened to be a good friend, and explained my situation. I suggested this would be a great opportunity to demo that eighty-thousand-dollar camera he had sitting on the shelf. He was ecstatic and, without hesitation, offered to ship the camera overnight, at his cost, to my hotel in Chicago. I got to the hotel the following day, just a few hours after the camera arrived. That evening, about twelve hours before the interview, I sat on the edge of the bed, carefully unpacked the camera, and read the instructions for the very first time. I had never used a sophisticated piece of equipment like it before. I don't know if I was more nervous about the interview or about mishandling and breaking the camera.

I stayed up most of the night with a caffeinated drink in one hand and the camera's owner's manual in the other, learning how to run the camera, giving myself lots of positive self-talk, and practicing until I looked like I had done hundreds of interviews.

The next morning, trembling but oddly confident, I filmed the interview with Gene Simmons of KISS. It was one of the most thrilling experiences of my life. Charrie and I had done our first *Turn Up The Volume!* interview. I am convinced God helped me that day because the camera worked perfectly and the interview was everything we hoped it would be.

Just as we planned, the Gene Simmons video ended up being sold in music stores throughout the country for several years. We went on to interview Jon Bon Jovi, Ozzy Osbourne, and many other rock stars. That one experience with Gene Simmons opened many doors and had an astonishing impact on my career. Twenty-five years later, Charrie is still my dear friend.

When I look back on it, I really had no business shooting that interview. I didn't have a camera, didn't have the resources to buy a camera, and didn't have the expertise to run the camera. But because Charrie believed in my idea and arranged the opportunity for me, failure was not an option. As soon as I hung up from that first call from Charrie, I could have curled up into a ball, but I remembered my grandfather's optimism and knew it was time to take one of his mottos to heart: Go, Baby, Go!

Staying up all night learning to run that camera was a Fake It Till You Make It moment. As far as Gene Simmons knew, I was an experienced cameraman, someone who knew what he was doing. I had an unusual sense of confidence that night in the hotel as I taught myself to run the camera. I had that confidence in part because I took the time to prepare. Charrie had put her reputation on the line for me to deliver, and so I did.

When we Fake It Till We Make It, we act with confidence, competence, and optimism, even if we don't feel all that confident, competent, or optimistic. *Act as if* you are already what you want to become. The morning I filmed Gene Simmons, I *acted as if* I was a seasoned, professional cameraman who knew exactly what he was doing, and Gene never suspected otherwise. Because I acted the part, an extraordinary thing happened. I started to believe it myself. By the time the interview was over, I had truly become a seasoned professional.

A CHRISTMAS CHALLENGE

One day during a college class, my professor told us he had funded the printing of a high quality coffee table Christmas book. For some reason I can't remember, the books had been pulled from bookstore shelves, and my professor had a storage unit full of books. I remember thinking there was an opportunity to make some money. After class, I approached the professor and asked if I could buy his inventory. He was thrilled, and I ended up with several cases of Christmas books to sell.

I went door to door to businesses in the area and explained that the books would be a great Christmas gift for employees. My sales pitch worked. I sold all of the books in a few weeks and made a great profit.

At one business, I sold a case of books to the marketing director, Tim Brown. Later Tim hired my video company to do some projects for him. Thirty years later, we still regularly go to lunch and concerts together. It all started from the Christmas book sale. My grandpa would have been proud.

There have been many times in my relationships, my career, and my musical experiences where I've gotten involved in something extraordinary and stepped back to ask myself, "What did you get yourself into? Can you deliver?" But I've usually found a way to make it happen.

I call this **The Turn Up the Volume Principle**: *Prepare, then fake it till you make it.*

Be ready when opportunities come, and don't let fear keep you from taking a chance.

JAMES JORDAN AND A PAIR OF SHOES

In 1993, the NBA All-Star Weekend was held in Salt Lake City. Big corporate sponsors hosted their own events as part of the main event. My production company was hired to shadow VIPs and corporate executives and take videos so they would have a personal memento of the weekend. I had access to almost anywhere I wanted to go.

My brother Mark is a big sports fan, so I invited him to tag along and help carry my equipment. The two of us got to hang around team owners and executives, and we met several NBA players. We brought basketballs with us and, like wide-eyed kids, asked players for their autographs.

This was the year the Chicago Bulls earned their first "three-peat," and Michael Jordan was at the peak of his professional career. Later that year, he would retire to play baseball. Along with the basketballs, my brother brought some Air Jordan shoes, replicas of the ones Jordan wore in the 1992 Summer Olympics in Barcelona, Spain. Jordan was part of the famous Olympic "Dream Team" that included basketball greats Larry Bird, Magic Johnson, and David Robinson. Nike made a limited run of the shoes with Jordan's Olympic number on them. The shoes my brother owned weren't the very shoes Jordan had worn, but they were exact replicas of his Olympic shoe, down to the size and style, and there had been very few produced. My brother lugged them everywhere we went on the slim chance we might run into Michael Jordan and get a signature.

On the night before the All-Star game, we went to an exclusive dinner for guests of the players. All sorts of basketball VIPs attended. There were some open seats at our table, and three people asked if they could join us. We made introductions and found out our table guests were Michael Jordan's wife, mother, and father. My brother's eyes got as big as the dinner plates on the table. He leaned toward me and whispered, "This is probably as close as we're going to get to Michael Jordan. Should we have his dad sign these shoes?"

"Let's do it," I said. We took out the shoes, and Michael Jordan's dad, James, cheerfully signed both of them: *James Jordan, Michael's dad.*

My brother saw a possibility and didn't let fear deter him from hauling those shoes around all weekend. He was prepared when the opportunity presented itself. Due to his tenacity and the generosity of James Jordan, we have a keepsake we still cherish.

When you're proactive—Go, Baby, Go—even if you're in over your head, fake it till you make it. Good things tend to happen.

MY MOM WAS NOT EATEN BY A BEAR

Fake It Till You Make It works even in the most unexpected places. A couple of years ago, I was in Montana visiting my elderly mother. My mom, my older brother Mark, and I went out to enjoy some time by the lake. Mark sat on the dock, and Mom and I sat on camping chairs farther back on the shore. My brother turned to say something to us, and his eyes nearly popped out of his head. "There's a bear behind you," he muttered. I slowly turned around, and sure enough, a bear sat watching us from about ten yards away. My mind quickly ran through my options for escape, most of which were not all that appealing with my ninety-year-old mother.

The good news was that I was an Eagle Scout, so I'd actually been prepared for a situation like this. The first reaction most people have when they meet a bear is to run. This is a very bad idea because the bear may consider you prey and take chase. Most people can't outrun a bear—certainly not my mom. A better option when encountering a bear is to curl up in a little ball and play dead. This usually works because the bear isn't interested in something that's already dead. This was a less appealing option with my mom, because I didn't know how easily she could get down on the ground and we might have had to curl up for a while.

I knew another option to deal with a bear is to try to scare it away by making a lot of noise and acting aggressively. Protecting my mom was my first priority, so I decided to fake it with the bear. I stood up, stretched my arms into the air, and started yelling at the top of my lungs, "Hey, bear! Hey, bear!" The bear licked his chops, turned around, and ambled away from us.

My mom's nickname was "Mamarazzi." She wasn't even fazed. She just wanted me to snap a photo as the bear walked away.

My brother wasn't so lucky. He wanted to get that photo for my mom, so he ran around the house to get closer to the bear. The bear charged at him, and Mark backed off. Soon the bear lost interest and lumbered back into the woods. Unfortunately, it was a "code brown" moment for Mark. He had to go in the house and change his pants.

In life, we're faced with all sorts of lions and tigers and bears—problems and setbacks that can terrify us and knock us to the ground. Do we run, curl up into a ball, or confront our fears? When challenges arise, stand up, be strong, and meet your troubles head on. You can conquer just about anything if you'll just face it. Go, Baby Go!

DON'T DO IT IF YOU SHOULDN'T

Faking it till you make it can get you into serious trouble if you're unprepared or if you fail to understand your limits.

Early in my video production career, ESPN asked me to direct a ski video. As was always the case in those early years, any paying project was welcome. And this was ESPN! They asked if I was a good skier, and I assured them I was, even though I hadn't snow-skied in years. I really needed the work, and I figured I could bluff my way through the skiing part. Fake It Till You Make It, right?

When we got to the ski resort, I was stunned by the skiing talent that had been assembled for the project. Before we started, the ski patrol guide asked, "Is everyone here an expert skier?" Everyone, including me, nodded in the affirmative. "We're going into the back country," the guide said. "It will be dangerous. You shouldn't be up there if you can't handle it."

Gulp.

I was the one in charge that day. It was a complex, multi-camera shoot, and I had been hired to direct the cameras. I *had* to be there even though it was obvious I was in over my head. Not only would

I be skiing in places I had no business being, but I had to direct the work of three cameras. Backing out at that stage of the project was not an option. I took a deep breath, forced a smile, and followed the guide into the back country.

An hour later, I found myself on some of the most treacherous and precarious slopes in the Wasatch Mountains, and I had no idea how to maneuver in the snow. Not only were we on incredibly steep slopes, but we were in deep powder, filming in ungroomed, untouched areas to get the beautiful shots the project called for. I not only put my own life at risk, but everyone else on the mountain as well.

I almost killed myself on that mountain. At least it felt that way.

Because it was a multi-day job, I came home after the first day and found an expert skier to take over the project. It cost me a lot of money, and ESPN never did business with my company again. After that, I turned down projects I knew I didn't have the ability to pull off. It was a lesson in wisdom and restraint I'll never forget.

For most of us, overconfidence is not the problem. More often, being timid and overly cautious is what holds us back from reaching our full potential. Fake It Till You Make It is the mantra that pulls us from our fears, our doubts, our couches, and inspires us to jump into the unknown and achieve phenomenal success. With preparation, Fake It Till You Make It gets us out of our own way so we can actually accomplish our most cherished goals and live fuller, richer lives.

POSTURE, CONFIDENCE, AND BODY CHEMISTRY

In her popular 2012 TED talk, Amy Cuddy, a Harvard Business School social psychologist, shared her research that adopting a powerful posture improves your body chemistry. In her study, she asked people to adopt either a power stance, with their chests and head lifted and arms propped on their hips, or a meeker pose, hunched over with their arms crossed, for two minutes. Those who maintained power poses showed a decrease in the stress hormone cortisol and an increase in testosterone, a hormone related to dominance and confidence. "Our nonverbal actions govern how we think and feel about ourselves," Cuddy concluded. "Our bodies change our minds."[13]

Other studies show that when you're placed in an unfamiliar situation, such as a new job, a different school, or an interview with Gene Simmons, the best thing you can do is copy a person who already possesses the required skills. Organizational behavior professor Herminia Ibarra writes in the *Harvard Business Review*, "By viewing ourselves as works in progress, we multiply our capacity to learn, avoid being pigeonholed, and ultimately become better leaders...We're never too experienced to fake it till we learn it."[14]

My grandfather lived by *The Turn Up the Volume Principle*. Fake It Till You Make It. Go, Baby, Go. He believed if he was prepared and took action, good things would come to him. I have consistently found this to be true. When in doubt, act.

THE TURN UP THE VOLUME PRINCIPLE

Prepare, then fake it till you make it.

Why was Indiana Jones willing to step off the ledge?

Because He Believed He Could Find a Way

"**W****hat do you want to be when you grow up?**"
My friend's eight-year-old daughter is still deciding her future. She either wants to be president of
the United States or a hairdresser. Regardless of what she chooses,
she knows this great truth: she can't be the president or a hairdresser without first believing she can.

In the movie *Indiana Jones and the Last Crusade*, Indiana Jones
and his father, Professor Henry Jones, are on a quest to find the
Holy Grail, the cup that Jesus was said to have used at the Last
Supper. Henry advises his son that to reach the Grail, one must pass
three tests. The most terrifying test requires Indiana Jones to cross
an apparently impassable and wide ravine. Indiana fears he will fall

to his death if he steps blindly into thin air, but his father is dying and he has run out of time. Henry urges Indiana to take a leap of faith. "You must believe, boy. You must believe," Henry implores.

Indiana closes his eyes and steps off the ledge into the ravine. He expects to fall, but instead, his foot lands on a stone path camouflaged by the walls of the ravine. Only after he steps into the emptiness of the ravine does the stone path appear. This "leap of faith" saves Indiana's father and is also symbolic of life.

Most of the important things we do in life take faith. Martin Luther King, Jr. said, "Faith is taking the first step even when you don't see the whole staircase."[15]

Dr. King was describing what I call **The Leap of Faith Principle:** *You act with faith when you take a courageous step into the unknown.*

Faith is not a sure knowledge. It is a firm belief in something for which there is no proof. We have faith when we believe we can find a way and then move into the dark. Faith is hope put into action.

When we embark on a journey, start a project, form a new relationship, create a new business, or take a risk in the business we're already in, we have no guarantee our efforts will prove successful or even that the effort will be worth the time. Like Indiana Jones, we are often taking steps into the unknown. We act, not because we know, but because we hope we can succeed and believe we can find a way.

When Dr. Myron Wentz started USANA, his professional career had been primarily in developing test kits to diagnose disease. He had enjoyed success as a scientist and a researcher and had a strong sense of what he wanted USANA to become. He used his vision to guide the company's growth, operating with confidence and hope that his vision would become a reality.

MEETING THE LOVE OF MY LIFE

When I met Lori Lynn Barber, she was an eighteen year old just out of high school. I was enchanted by her good looks, her brains, and her spunk. We were both going to a small college in Idaho, and we had similar interests, spent a lot of time together, and became good friends. I grew increasingly fond of Lori and wanted her to feel the same about me, but there was a problem: Lori had a serious boyfriend, and I knew if I was going to win her heart, I had to be extraordinary and extraordinarily creative.

I wanted to do something on our first date to show her how interested I was. Not far from the college were some ice caves originally formed hundreds of thousands of years ago. The caves stay frozen all year and make for an awesome place to explore and have some fun. I thought it would be the perfect place for my first date with Lori. We went on a double date. My roommate and I went ahead of time and left my guitar, some chairs, and tinfoil dinners outside the caves. We also prepared a fire pit with plenty of wood. After we wandered around the caves for a while, we went outside to a cooked meal. Lori was surprised and very impressed.

I was competing for Lori's love, so I planned activities that went above and beyond normal dates. On another date, I got permission to use the science lab on campus. We put on safety glasses and had goulash in the lab. I set up the lab so our drinks were dispensed down test tubes and into beakers.

I was playing in the college jazz band at the time, and I had keys to the music room. My musician friends and I would take our dates to the music room, teach each person how to play a part on a random instrument, and form our own rock band. We managed to come up with all sorts of creative activities.

I finally convinced Lori to marry me, and we still enjoy creative dates. On one date, a friend and I sent our wives on a scavenger hunt that ended at a dance club. We had western clothing ready, and a dance instructor gave us private dancing lessons.

We spent our 30th anniversary in our RV in the Walmart parking lot because Walmart allows RVs to park for free. Lori teased me that I really showed her a good time camping at Walmart on her anniversary. On that trip, our kids accused us of being old people so we went to a local second-hand store and bought several leisure suits. In every picture we sent home to our kids, we dressed in a different leisure suit. In hopes of embarrassing our children, we made a music video of our anniversary trip—complete with every leisure suit we had purchased.

I can't begin to describe how much I love Lori or what a pillar of strength she has been to me during our thirty-plus years of marriage. I am the man I am, to a great degree, because of her example, her friendship, and her love for me. She's an incredible wife and a great support to our children. I am so glad Lori made a leap of faith by taking a chance on a skinny drummer from Montana who had big dreams.

HOPE AND THE UNCERTAINTY OF WAR

Hope, faith's companion, is believing things will work out.

My dad met my mom at a dance. As my mom tells it, it was raining hard that night, and my dad and his friends had a car and offered Mom and her friends a ride home. The girls squeezed into the car, and Mom ended up on Dad's lap. Their love story began.

My dad joined the merchant marine and married my mom shortly thereafter. Then he, like so many other young men of that generation, was called up to fight in the war. I can't imagine the emotions my mom must have experienced as her new husband left for war. She had nothing but her faith, her family, and her hope to sustain her.

My dad was assigned to a huge oil tanker that refueled battleships and freighters in the Pacific Theater. Both the Germans and Japanese targeted oil tankers in an effort to cut off supply lines for the Navy. They sank hundreds of American cargo ships, killed more than 18,000 American merchant mariners, and sent tons of vital supplies to the bottom of the oceans. Dad spent the majority of the war supplying the battleships in some of the most dangerous encounters that took place in the Asia Pacific.

Although he talked very little about the war, he occasionally shared insights he learned from the experience. He acted on faith that he would return to his bride to start a family. Faith isn't about *what is*, but rather a belief and hope in *what can be.* Dad's vision of the future kept him going during some very dangerous times.

Another story I often share about maintaining belief and holding onto hope comes from James Stockdale, a Vietnam War prison camp survivor.

While flying a mission, Commander James Stockdale's jet was shot down over North Vietnam. He parachuted into a small village where he was taken captive, brutally beaten, and held at the infamous Hanoi Hilton for seven and a half years. He was locked in leg irons in a bath stall and routinely tortured and beaten. In the book *Good to Great*, Jim Collins shares a conversation he had with Stockdale about how he was able to survive that horrible experience. Stockdale explained, "I never lost faith in the end of the story, I never doubted not only that I would get out, but also that I would prevail in the end and turn the experience into the defining event of my life, which, in retrospect, I would not trade."

Collins was curious about the prisoners who didn't make it out of Vietnam alive. "Oh, they were the ones who said, 'We're going to be out by Christmas.' And Christmas would come, and Christmas would go. Then they'd say, 'We're going to be out by Easter.' And Easter would come, and Easter would go. And then Thanksgiving, and then it would be Christmas again. And they died of a broken heart...This is a very important lesson."[16] Collins described this philosophy as the "Stockdale Paradox": Having faith that things will work out but accepting what Collins calls "the brutal facts."

This paradox rings true with so many challenges we face in life and business. Whether it's a bad business decision, addiction, divorce, grief over the loss of a loved one, or a host of other difficulties, "You have to have faith that you will prevail in the end, regardless of the difficulties, *and at the same time,* you must confront the most brutal facts of your current reality, whatever they might be."[17]

MOVE FORWARD, EVEN WHEN YOU CAN'T SEE WHAT LIES AHEAD

When Collin Raye asked me to play with his band for the first time, there was no time for a rehearsal. I arrived in Florida shortly before we went on stage, and I was concerned how I would perform. When I shared my anxiety with Collin, he put his arm around my shoulders, looked me in the eye, and said, "You'll do just fine, Kevin." The assurance he expressed gave me the confidence I needed to get the job done. I accepted the brutal facts of the moment, said a prayer, told myself I could do it, and played my heart out. Hope, in part, is moving forward, even when you can't quite see what lies ahead. Like Indiana Jones, it's taking that step, even if the outcome is uncertain.

In *The 7 Habits of Highly Effective People*, Stephen R. Covey identifies Habit 2 as *Begin With the End in Mind.* Habit 2 is about the ability to envision what does not yet exist—the idea that all things are created twice. First is the mental creation (an idea), and second is the physical creation (making the idea real). The physical creation follows the mental, just as the construction of a house follows the drawing of a blueprint. Exercising faith means to begin each day, each task, each project with a clear vision of your desired direction and destination and then to continue by being proactive to make things happen.[18]

Belief, hope, and faith are foundations for happiness, peace of mind, and long-term success. Some people say these are spiritual qualities, and I believe they are. It is because of my spiritual beliefs I do much of what I do. I am able to survive difficult times knowing that if I do my part, things will ultimately work out for the better. This belief guides me to take action. Belief, hope, and faith are also foundational qualities for anyone who is doing the hard work of turning mental creation into physical creation. Dr. Wentz never would have succeeded had he not had the belief, faith, and confidence things would work out.

Having faith always involves dealing with risk. Risk can produce great rewards. Facebook founder Mark Zuckerberg says, "The biggest risk is not taking any risk...In a world that is changing really quickly, the only strategy that is guaranteed to fail is not taking risks."[19]

How many business ideas never materialized because of fear? Taking a risk, taking a leap of faith, is an essential part of progress.

Hope and faith are action words. We can't sit around and do nothing if we want hope and faith to work in our lives. People without faith, either in themselves or others, don't seem to get much done. They're undecided, doubtful. They refuse to act, and good things seldom happen to them. On the other hand, people who have faith tend to act. They take risks and move forward with hope, enthusiasm, and confidence that things will work out.

Brad Henry, former Governor of Oklahoma, said, "Believe in yourself, and the rest will fall into place. Have faith in your own abilities, work hard, and there is nothing you cannot accomplish." [20] Having faith and belief in yourself is one of the fundamental keys to success and happiness.

Tim Brown, the marketing director who bought my Christmas books, lost his job because his employer's company was acquired and the new company eliminated his position. Tim immediately found another job as a public relations executive, but nine months later when he and his wife were expecting their fifth child, his position was eliminated due to downsizing. During those months of unemployment, he dug deeply into his faith and wrote the following:

THINGS WILL WORK OUT

Things will work out,
They always do.
Rough times come,
That's nothing new.

But how you view it
What you see,
Guides you to where
You'll eventually be.

So, decide where it is
That will make it just right.
Then skirt all thoughts
That veer from your sight.

Because times do get rough,
That's nothing new,
But things will work out...
They always do.

Two months later, Tim was hired by a major advertising agency and worked there for nearly thirty years. Things *will* work out. You must believe. Faith is the power that moves you forward.

THE LEAP OF FAITH PRINCIPLE

You act with faith when you take
a courageous step into the unknown.

Why did Tommy Shaw perform in a bowling alley?

Because He Wanted To Be Ready

I gingerly cradled the stone, **The Queen of Diamonds, in my** hand. It was about the size of a walnut and heavier than I would have expected. Carefully, I rolled the fabled gem from side to side in my hand as sparks of light flashed from its depths. Even knowing that diamonds are the hardest natural material on earth, I was fearful of dropping it. How had a kid from Montana found his way into the inner vault of one of the most heavily guarded buildings in the country?

The most famous diamond in the world is the Hope Diamond, also known as *Le Bijou du Roi* (the King's Jewel). It is a forty-five-and-a-half carat, deep blue diamond housed in the National Gem and Mineral collection at the Smithsonian National Museum of

Natural History in Washington, D.C. When exposed to ultraviolet light, the Hope Diamond glows with a brilliant red phosphorescence that makes it seem the stone is filled with blood. The eerie red glow I witnessed first-hand helps scientists "fingerprint" blue diamonds, allowing them to tell real ones from fake. The unnerving, tawny radiance of the diamond persists for some time after the ultraviolet light is removed. The bizarre glowing quality of the stone, along with a number of strange occurrences in relation to it, have fueled the diamond's reputation for being cursed.

According to legend, the Hope Diamond brings misfortune and tragedy to anyone who touches it. But there is also convincing evidence that such stories have been fabricated to enhance the stone's mystery and appeal, since increased publicity often raises a gem's value. Nevertheless, I hesitated briefly when I was given the opportunity to hold it for a photo shoot. Legends can be powerful.

Early in my career as a video producer and not long after I graduated from college, I had far more expenses than I had income. Lori and I had two children, and Lori was a stay-at-home mom. At the time, few things mattered more than making money and keeping our family afloat. My goal was to make my own videos so I had the rights of ownership and could collect residual income off royalties.

A good friend of mine, Ray Albrechtsen, came up with the idea of partnering with the Smithsonian Institute on educational video projects. About twenty-five million people visit the Smithsonian every year. We calculated that if we could get videos featuring the museum into the Smithsonian gift shops, we could make a great deal of money. This was before the time of DVDs, and many tourists wanted a video souvenir of their Smithsonian experiences. We also thought a video on the Hope Diamond would be popular in gem stores throughout the country.

Ray was a geology fanatic and had several contacts in the gemstone world. Through his tireless legwork, we made a connection with the curator-in-charge of the Smithsonian Institute's Gem and Mineral Collection. The curator oversaw the many gleaming specimens and million-dollar jewels that have found a home in the Institute's famous Gem Hall. Among the thousands of pieces in the National Gem and Mineral collection, the most sought-after is the storied Hope Diamond.

After many letters, proposals, and a multitude of phone calls, we were about ready to give up. Progress was too slow, and coming to an agreement proved almost impossible. But our work finally paid off. We were invited to come to the Institute for a meeting.

The invitation couldn't have come at a better time. I was doing some work for STS Productions, which was owned by American Stores, and they had a private jet. At that time, I had never seen a private jet before, let alone flown on one. STS Productions flew us to Washington, and again I asked myself, "How did a kid from Montana with rock 'n' roll dreams end up on a private jet on a trip to the Smithsonian Institute?"

It was clear during our meeting that the curator was a preeminent gem expert. He knew almost everything there was to know about the gemstones in the Smithsonian collection, as well as the history of any stone or piece we asked about. We immediately connected with him, and within minutes, it felt like we were old friends. After showing us Gem Hall, the curator invited us into the vaults where they kept most of the precious stones and other jewelry not on display. The vaults were both astonishing and overwhelming.

A person could spend weeks touring the public areas of the Smithsonian Institute and not see all there is to see, but there are many more artifacts and precious objects in the vaults not accessible to the public. That afternoon in the vaults, we barely scratched the surface of what the Smithsonian has in storage in its gem and mineral collection.

With a smile on his face, the curator warned us about the curse of the diamond, suggesting we might want to drive back to Utah instead of fly. He let us handle the Hope Diamond for as long as we wanted and gave us permission to take pictures holding the precious jewel. To make sure we were doubly impressed, he turned off the regular lights and turned on the black light to "power it up." The diamond glowed blood red in the darkness long after the black light was turned off. I enjoyed every minute, doubting I would ever hold something of that value in my hand again.

We ended up making the Smithsonian gemstone video and a few others. The first video about gemstones of America was produced by STS Productions and narrated by Efrem Zimbalist Jr., a famous TV personality. Just as we hoped, tourists bought thousands of copies at the Smithsonian Museum stores and in other gift shops around the country.

Some of my friends told me how lucky I was to have been able to be part of such a deal, and they were at least partly correct. There probably was some luck involved. It was a real Fake It Till You Make It experience. But luck wasn't the only reason I got to hold the Hope Diamond; anyone involved in the project would tell you we put in hours of hard work to get there. Luck tends to favor people who are prepared when it shows up.

I've come to live according to **The Hope Diamond Principle:** *Good things come to those who are prepared.*

You can't depend on luck. You need to be ready for opportunities that might come your way.

IS THERE A BASS PLAYER IN THE HOUSE?

In *The 7 Habits of Highly Effective People,* Habit 1 is **Be Proactive**.[21] Proactivity is looking forward, anticipating, preparing. It's knowing where you want to go and developing the mental attitude and necessary skills to get there before you even start the journey. Being proactive requires two things: 1) knowing what you want, and 2) doing the work beforehand to take advantage when the opportunity arrives.

As a teenager, I went to concerts and dreamed of performing with whatever band was on stage. One of my fantasies was that one of the musicians would get sick or wouldn't be able to perform, and in crisis, the lead singer would shout into the crowd, "Is there anybody out there who knows how to play our music?" I dreamed of volunteering to play, jumping up on the stage, and saving the concert. I've always wanted to be ready to play if they needed me. The desire to be prepared drove me to practice.

My desire to always be ready spilled into other areas of my life. In college, I became interested in learning all there was to know about video production, and I paid the price to learn. I gave up nights and weekends to take part in productions and video shoots. Even if I didn't get paid, I knew I was gaining skills and moving in the right direction. When I eventually started my own production business, we succeeded, in part, because I was ready.

Before USANA bought my production company, I realized I needed additional skills in business management, leadership, and personal development. I became a voracious reader on these subjects. I read business books and attended personal development

workshops that didn't have much to do with music or video production, because I wanted to be ready. I recognized I might have the
opportunity to take a more central role in a company someday.

During this intense study, I became acquainted with Denis
Waitley's philosophy on winning and serving others, and his ideas
rang true to me. For over twenty years, Denis has been one of my
mentors and dearest friends. I have listened to or read everything
he has written and produced, and he has taught me a tremendous
amount about success.

I have made a habit of continually reading personal growth
books. You never know when an opportunity will arise.

NIGHTCLUBS AND BOWLING ALLEYS

Like me, Tommy Shaw loved music and played and sang anywhere
he could get work. He played with one band in an obscure nightclub
in Chicago for a brief period of time. After Chicago, Tommy went to
Alabama where he played in a bowling alley bar with a couple of his
friends. Playing nights at a bowling alley, Tommy probably thought
his music career had stalled out.

The band Styx was getting ready to embark on a nationwide tour,
but at the last minute, their lead vocalist unexpectedly left the band.
They began a frantic search for a replacement. Someone influential
with Styx had heard Tommy sing in Chicago and thought he might
be a good fit with the band. They listened to his demo tape and were
impressed with his vocal range. Tommy's life changed forever when
Styx invited him to join the band, but what if he hadn't been ready
when that incredible opportunity arrived?

When I was in high school, I was a big fan of Styx. Styx was a
hugely popular band in the 1970s and 1980s. They had four consec-
utive multi-platinum albums and sixteen top-40 singles in the U.S.

I idolized their lead singer, Tommy Shaw, and alongside the posters of Gene Simmons and KISS, I hung posters of Styx and Tommy Shaw in my room. Tommy was my idol. When other kids were outside playing ball, I was learning his songs—*Renegade, Crystal Ball, Too Much Time on My Hands*. At my first paying job as a musician, we played some of his songs.

A few years ago at a USANA event, I had the opportunity to play with Tommy Shaw in front of thousands of people. To say that was a thrill is an understatement. It was a teenage dream come true. I have also had the opportunity to play with Kenny Loggins, Belinda Carlisle, and Eddie Money. I never could have played at that level if I hadn't been prepared. Maybe I got lucky. Or maybe I had been ready all my life to seize the opportunities that came my way.

I've come to realize that you never know what opportunities are going to present themselves. That's why you have to be ready.

Had I not been learning, investing in myself, going to John Maxwell trainings in California, attending workshops on my own dime, reading and studying, taking internet courses, and wanting to improve, I doubt I would have had the amazing leadership opportunities that eventually came my way at USANA. Many people aren't ready to take advantage of big chances, and they miss out.

Opportunities are always there for the prepared.

THE HOPE DIAMOND PRINCIPLE

Good things come to those who are prepared.

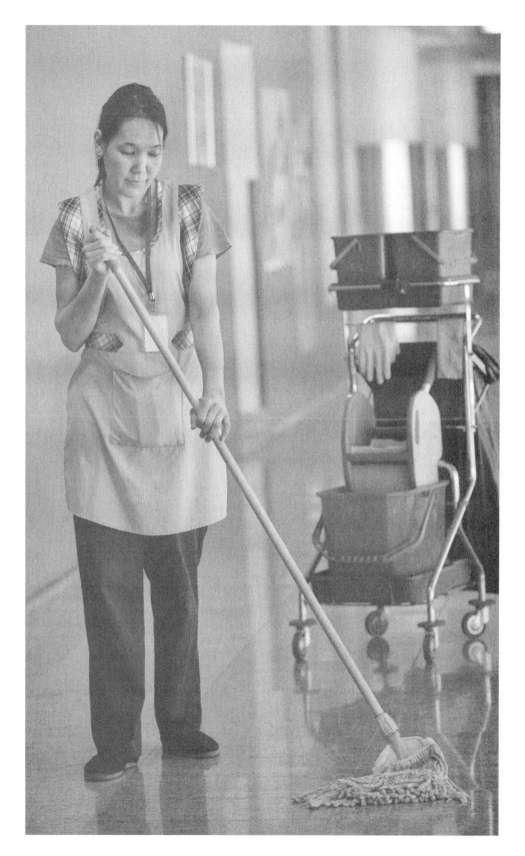

*Why did the professor ask his students
to learn the cleaning lady's name?*

Because Nothing
Is More Important
Than Relationships

O n the first day of class, one of my college professors wrote on the board, "*Nothing is more important than relationships.*"

To a young college kid, it seemed a strange way to start the class and maybe a little unnecessary. At that point, grades seemed more important than relationships. Learning seemed more important than relationships. Graduating seemed a lot more important than everything else.

I spent hours studying for the final exam, but on test day our professor surprised us. "The final exam has one question. What did

I write on the board the first day of class?" More than thirty years later, I still remember my professor and that class. "Nothing is more important than relationships."

There is a story of a young college student whose professor gave his class a pop quiz a few weeks into the semester. The student breezed through the test until he got to the last question: "What is the name of the woman who cleans this building?" The student wondered if the question was a joke. He'd seen the cleaning woman several times during those first weeks of school quietly going about her business, making sure the halls and rooms were clean for the students. She was tall with dark hair, in her mid-fifties, but other than that, the student hadn't paid much attention to her. Why would he know her name? The student stewed for a while then handed in the test with the last question blank.

One bewildered student asked if the question would count toward their grade.

"Absolutely," the professor said. "In your careers, your paths will cross with many people. They all matter and deserve your attention and care, even if all you do is smile, say hello, and learn their names. Few things are more important to people than being called by their first name." It didn't take everyone in the class long to learn who the cleaning lady was. Her name was Dorothy.[22]

I came to understand the importance of relationships not only from my professor, but also by watching my parents. Mom and Dad had many close friends, and some of those friendships spanned decades. Maybe their concern for others was nurtured by growing up in a small town where people watched out for each other. Maybe they simply saw how vital friendships are to a rich and fulfilling life.

Dad was the first to help a neighbor who needed him, and he often took his boys along. He helped friends build and repair homes, helped when the church needed an addition, helped people with all sorts of repairs. As his sons, we were expected to go along with him. He was an extraordinary example of service.

My dad always focused on how he could give instead of what he could get. His greatest desire was to do good. My dad helped my oldest brother LaMar build his own house. Every day after school when I didn't have something else going on, I was expected to go with my dad and help on the house. Many days we worked late into the night, even in the freezing cold. I didn't especially like helping Dad with his projects, but he taught me a valuable lesson about service and relationships I will never forget.

My parents cherished and nurtured close relationships, and the high priority they placed on those relationships stuck with me. Few things are more important to me than my relationships, both within the company and in other areas of my life.

I want you to remember **The Dorothy Principle**: *Nothing is more important than relationships.*

LAKES AND SAWMILLS

The Flathead Valley in Montana where I grew up sits at the base of the Rocky Mountains near Glacier National Park, one of the most majestic settings in North America. The valley is surrounded by spectacular, glacier-encrusted mountains, carpeted with miles of lush pine forests, and dotted with dozens of pristine, clear lakes. With plentiful water and sunlight, many of the trees grow as tall as 170 feet and six feet in diameter. A number of sawmills in the area transformed the mammoth trees into millions of board feet of lumber that was shipped all around the world.

My dad started out as a bookkeeper for Superior Buildings Lumber Company, and he became such a valued employee that the owner of the lumber company gave him a small percentage of the business as a gift. The owner, Mr. Crum, got too old to run the business, and his family eventually put him in a nursing home. My dad visited the nursing home every other day, shaving and taking care of Mr. Crum until the day he died. When Dad couldn't make it, my brother LaMar would go instead. Dad was like an adopted son to the Crum family because of all the service he rendered them over the years.

When Mr. Crum passed away, my dad and a coworker bought the lumber company. Growing up, I did a lot of work at that sawmill.

Shortly after Lori and I married, Dad got me a job at the mill. I remember my first day on the job: I sort of hoped to be given special treatment because I was the boss's kid. Boy, was I in for a shock. My dad introduced me to the foreman and said, "This is my son, and I want you to know you have my permission to fire him. I helped him get this job, but it's up to him to keep it." I almost had to work harder because my dad was the boss.

 Turning a twenty-five-ton tree into useable lumber is hazardous work. One of the dangerous assignments in a sawmill is at the end of the dry chain, where the boards end up after they've been cut and planed. It's the one job at the mill nobody wants. That's where they put the new guys to see if they're tough enough or dumb enough to endure the work.

The men at the end of the dry chain work outside of the building, collecting, sorting, and stacking the newly milled lumber. In the summer, it is miserably hot and in the winter, horribly cold.

Today's sawmills use automatic systems to do this work, but back then, it was all manual labor. This was where I started my short-lived career at the sawmill. It was one of the most miserable jobs I've ever had, and that first ten-hour shift working the dry chain was one of the longest days of my life.

The mill supervisor was a gruff man, but he and I became friends, not because of my dad's position, but because we got along so well. One day, I made a mistake on the dry chain, and they had to shut down the whole plant to fix it. The supervisor was patient with me in his own way and took the time to teach me what I'd done wrong. He became something of a mentor to me. We often talked about my future, and he told me that working at a sawmill was not the kind of life I wanted and there were preferable ways to earn a living. Because he wanted me to have a better life, he emphasized the importance of getting an education.

I came to appreciate how important relationships are, especially with people who share their wisdom and point you in a better direction.

Starting in eighth grade, my band began playing around the valley. We were pretty good. We could play Tom Petty, Styx, KISS, The Beatles, Led Zeppelin, and a few Deep Purple songs. The first place we ever played was at a house party. Someone called the police, and the party got shut down. Our brush with the law did not deter our band. I learned that the person who owns the sound system is the one who makes the decisions, negotiates the contracts, and runs the business. I bought the equipment and became the band's self-appointed leader and business manager. With my parents' full support, we practiced at my house, sometimes for hours a day.

The high schools in the valley had regular dances after the football games. We played at many of them and started making good money. The regular gigs gave us confidence and increased our ability to play together. I was just a school kid but had already learned that our band's success was as much about who we knew as it was about how good we were.

GETTING GOOD COUNSEL FROM TRUSTED FRIENDS

One autumn afternoon, I was called to the principal's office. The principal told me the school district could no longer hire our band because the band members weren't part of the union. The principal and I were friends, and he didn't like giving me this news. He worried some of the teachers would encourage others to go on strike because the schools in the district were hiring our band. I was stunned. I had no understanding of union politics.

My dad's company was one of the few lumber companies in Montana that was not a union shop. It was a smaller business and unable to meet all the union's requirements. Joining the union would have put it out of business. When my dad heard our band's predicament, he was furious. We talked into the night and explored options.

Following my father's counsel, our band decided to join the Flathead Valley Musicians' Union. We were all fifteen years old, and a bunch of kids joining the union was unheard of. Fortunately, there were no rules against it, so they had to let us join. We filled out the paperwork, paid the dues, and became full-fledged members of the union. After that, we played at high school functions in the district with the full support of the union.

The head of the local musicians' union was a good man. It was easy to make friends with him because we both had a passion for music. Because of our friendship, our band wanted to help him with the business inside the union. The band came to union meetings and supported him with our votes. In return, he gave us the best gigs that came through the union. Even though we were friends, we never compromised our values or voted for things we didn't support. We helped each other in good and positive ways to make things better.

Because of the manager at the sawmill, the principal at my high school, and the head of the music union, I learned how to meet other people's needs, how to negotiate, and how to get things done by leveraging relationships. I learned how important it is to sincerely care about the people you do business with. Developing a genuine relationship will always pay big dividends, even if the payoff is simply having a deeper understanding of someone else.

When I started in college, I formed a band and immediately developed a personal relationship with the top booking agent for most of Utah and Wyoming. This agent loved Harley Davidson motorcycles. When I traveled, I made a special point to find the nearest Harley Davidson shop and get him a Harley t-shirt with the name of the city on it. When I paid him his cut of our band profits, I'd give him the Harley shirt. He loved those t-shirts, and we started getting better gigs.

Other bands often argued with our agent over commissions and tried to talk him down on his percentage cut. I did just the opposite. I gladly paid his fee and sometimes a bit more. We tended to get the most attractive and lucrative gigs, and we got all the work we could handle.

I LIKE TO LOOK YOU IN THE EYE

As human beings, we need each other. We need encouragement, empathy, and connections. We need smiles, kind words, good advice, and trusted friends. We need mentors and teachers and people who make us feel uncomfortable in our comfort zones. Sometimes we even need a kick in the seat of the pants. No matter who we are or how meager we think our abilities, we all have something to give our fellow humans. We all have specific talents or experiences we can use to bless someone else. Strong relationships are essential to a happy and successful life.

Having interacted with thousands of people during my career, I have come to realize that the best, most authentic relationship-building experiences happen when you're sitting kneecap to kneecap with someone, looking each other in the eye, and sincerely wanting to understand. Facebook, Instagram, email, Skype, and other forms of electronic media are great for communicating and connecting across distances, but face-to-face meetings lead to solid business partnerships and long-term relationships. These are the meaningful relationships that help grow a business. They foster trust, build bridges, and help us manage conflict from a position of mutual understanding. With all of its incredible benefits, technology can't replace the power of face-to-face communication.

Anyone who has spent time with me knows that when it comes to face-to-face communication, I am a big crybaby. I feel a deep emotional connection to my associates at work, and I am passionate about principles that are important to me. Sometimes those emotions tend to spill out through my eyes. I was eight or nine years old when my sister got married, and if my brothers are to be believed, my family couldn't hear the wedding ceremony because I was crying so hard. I didn't want to lose my sister.

Recently, a business situation arose in a country far from my home that required my involvement. It was close to Christmas, and I had already been traveling for three straight weeks. I didn't want to go anywhere so close to Christmas. I didn't want to fly halfway around the globe for what I expected to be a two-hour meeting. Couldn't I solve the problem sitting in my office in front of my computer in a virtual meeting? It would have been easy to talk myself out of that trip, but I paid attention to the distress signals and knew I must make the visit. My efforts to be there in person did not go unnoticed or unappreciated. The fact that I had traveled half-way across the world demonstrated my commitment to the company and the importance I placed on relationships. USANA's associates, in return, were more committed to finding a solution knowing I had come so far. We made much more progress than we would have communicating through the computer.

Technology is ideal for training and project management but falls short for building relationships and addressing conflict. The only way I can see to have authentic experiences with people is by connecting face-to-face. Be there. Immerse yourself in their company. Shake their hands. Don't rely on technology to do the critically important work of relationship building. Technology is handy, but being there is essential.

HOW DO YOU TREAT PEOPLE WHO HAVE NOTHING TO GIVE YOU?

With all my heart, I believe in the intrinsic value of each individual. Inspired by my parents' example, I have learned to truly care about people. This conscious concern for others has been a key to my personal success and happiness. I care deeply about the people at USANA, as well as everyone I have met in my many travels around the world. Regardless of background or nationality, race or creed, we are all on this journey together, and we must help each other along the way. We need each other.

A savvy, friendly Utah businesswoman was hired as a sales trainer at another nutritional supplement company. At her first company event, she stood at the entrance and eagerly introduced herself to everyone, hoping to get to know as many people in the company as she could. She introduced herself to a distributor and asked the distributor's name. The distributor, who turned out to be one of the company's top performers, frowned and said, "You don't know who I am? I'm too important at this company for you to not know who I am." Then she walked away. I'm guessing this "important" person didn't have many friends or close, trusting relationships at her company.

James D. Miles said, "You can easily judge the character of a man by how he treats those who can do nothing for him."[23]

It's a shift in thinking to look at someone and wonder, *Who is this person? What does he need and how can I help him?* I choose to be his friend and then act on those questions. A friend of mine calls me a chameleon because of my ability to mix with almost any type of person in almost any setting. I am just as comfortable with people in a pub as I am with people in church. The more you get to know people from different cultures and backgrounds, the more you come to appreciate the commonalities we share. People can bring incredible richness and joy to your life if you take the time to get to know them.

I recently met with 300 USANA salespeople, and during dinner, I did my best to shake hands with every person in the room. I wanted to look them all in the eye and let them know they were genuinely appreciated. Although I had previously met some of them, for many it was our first experience together. Shaking hands with 300 people in a few hours was exhausting, but I really wanted each of them to know how deeply I care about them.

FRIENDSHIP IN ANY LANGUAGE

Once I was interviewed by one of the most respected journalists in China. She works for a TV station whose viewing audience is much larger than anything in the United States. She also interviewed Vladimir Putin and regularly interviews the president of China. This was a very prestigious and important interview, and I felt the pressure to do well. I knew the interview could be very positive for the many people who were involved in USANA's business in China.

Before we recorded the interview, the reporter pulled me aside. "I want to spend a few minutes so I can get to know you before we get on camera. Let's sit down and chat." She was warm, genuine, and caring, and she made me feel like I was important to her, independent of the interview she was about to conduct. I can see why she is so successful. Her interest in me was sincere.

Prior to my interview, I was given a copy of the questions she would ask me, but because of our conversation before filming, she took the interview in a completely different direction. She spent the majority of time asking about my values and the values of our company. After the interview, she said she felt something different about me she didn't usually feel from people she interviewed. She didn't know if the difference was in USANA's purpose or my personal values, but she recognized a difference.

Part of what she felt came as a natural result of her efforts to understand me and the USANA business. The following day, a picture and a synopsis of the interview appeared on the front page of the largest newspaper in China. She recently sent me a holiday greeting and asked me how my family celebrates Christmas. I deeply appreciate her keeping in touch.

Winston Churchill is credited with saying, "You make a living out of what you get. You make a life out of what you give."[24] Many people enter relationships for what they think they can get instead of what they can give. If we were to focus more on the giving than getting, the return would be enormous.

OUR MOST IMPORTANT RELATIONSHIPS ARE IN OUR FAMILIES

My parents were dedicated to their family. My dad took us boys with him whenever he went out to help someone. When I was in grade school, my mom had a job to help pay the bills, and she and I would come home for lunch every day and watch "Bewitched" together while we ate. I always thought I was her favorite.

I knew my parents believed in me. They always supported my music. They didn't seem to mind having our band practice at their house, even though I'm sure the noise was overwhelming at times. My dad would often come home from work and start dancing to one of the songs we were playing. Before I got my driver's license, my mom and dad would drive our band to performances. Once they rented a trailer to haul our equipment to a city fifty miles away just so we could play. They stayed with us all night.

The day I turned fifteen, Mom drove me to my driver's test in our red Ford station wagon with wood paneling on the sides. I had loaded our car with band equipment, and as soon as I passed the test, I drove home, dropped Mom off, picked up my bandmates, and drove us to our next performance.

Theodore Hesburgh said, "The most important thing a father can do for his children is to love their mother."[25] Through five decades of marriage, my dad was an extraordinary example of this. If you wanted to get on the wrong side of my dad, you only had to do something to upset Mom. Dad would not tolerate anyone showing disrespect to our mother. I loved that about him. My mom passed

My first band, Alibi, honed our craft in my parents' basement. They were angels for lending us the room. We thought we were cooler than cool.

What does every kid need when he breaks his thumb? A delicious birthday cake from his grandma and grandpa.

When Grandpa wanted to share wisdom with his energetic grandson, I stopped and cherished the moments. I miss Grandpa and loved every minute with him.

74

I can't tell you how proud I am to call this 1944 beauty my mom. She glowed from the inside out and made everyone around her feel like they were the most important person in the world. Mom shaped my life, and I am forever grateful.

Such a classy couple. My parents had a look that said, "No matter what, we are going to make life wonderful." With that determination, how could they not be successful? My parents raised 5 children, and I was lucky enough to be one of them.

On my parents' 50th wedding anniversary, they were even more in love, holding hands and blessing lives with their generous hearts everywhere they went. I am lucky to call them Mom and Dad.

My favorite mode of transportation when I was doing church volunteer work for two years in the Netherlands.

I sometimes miss the forest surrounding my boyhood home. I was a happy kid. Why not?! Life is what you make it.

Where it all began. My two parents and four siblings shaped the young Kevin Guest, and I'll be forever grateful for my wonderful family.

Gene Simmons at my first "Turn Up the Volume" interview.

Backstage with Charrie Foglio, Bret Michaels, and my in-style acid-wash jeans.

When I was a teenager, I idolized Tommy Shaw (poster behind), had the world by the tail, and sometimes didn't bother to wear a shirt.

Even on the golf course, the legendary comedian Bob Hope made everyone laugh. That's probably how he got the best score.

Even at photo time, I was still shocked that I got to work with former U.S. President Gerald R. Ford. Sometimes luck finds you.

If you're ever going to launch your music CD sales in Walmart, wear a red shirt and hat. Shoppers love that.

In the glory days with Midnight Rodeo, I had good friends and a pretty decent mullet.

Behind locked doors holding the Hope Diamond.
I was in total awe.

Without a wonderful wife, I couldn't have
made it through college with a growing family.
It was the right plan at the right time, and we
wouldn't have had it any other way.

This picture of Mom and Dad on their
wedding day always warms my heart. It
shows love, respect, and commitment on that
day when promises were made and their
whole life was in front of them.
To me, it's inspiring.

I thought it then when Lori and I took our engagement picture, and I believe it even more now: I'm the luckiest guy in the world!

The wedding day. Our journey begins.

We're trying to be cool on a hot desert day with sunglasses and smiles.

My backyard at Lake Blaine in Montana. It has always been a place of peace and tranquility to help me think through life and be inspired. I've seen the world, but for me, there's no place more beautiful than home.

As a Pirate for the Day, I snatched the prettiest maiden
in the land. She may not look it here,
but that made her happy.

Whenever we can be together,
we cherish each moment and
every memory.

Lori is a master at dress-ups. We go "all out" and
always have a great time.

Lori and I regularly devote time to
our faith and love visiting beautiful
temples. Our visits remind us to be more
thoughtful friends and better people.

When my family gets together, we can't help
but have at least one goofy picture.

The beginnings of a wild party.

Being with family brings out the smiles, no matter where we travel.

A beautiful lake, a beautiful woman. The only thing left is a surprise kiss to make it a perfect day.

We find time to dance in the desert. Maybe we should all dance a little more. It's hard not to smile when you do.

Can you think of any better way to spend a lazy summer day? I have spent hours on this lake and loved every minute.

Stephani and Jess get married. Lori's mom and Stephani's namesake, Karen, joins the family picture.

All dressed in festive outfits with faces like that? This could be the beginning of mischief.

If you lose your horse on a desert hike, you know whom to turn to. Giddy up!

Alan Osmond, like each Osmond in that famous family, is as classy and professional as they come.

Exploring the beauty of Africa with two of my mentors, Dr. Wentz and Denis Waitley.

At my first Grand Ole Opry performance with Collin Raye, I was as nervous as the Opry was grand, but Collin calmed me with wise counsel.

Music legends Hank Williams, Garth Brooks, The Eagles, and countless other stars have performed in the Grand Ole Opry circle.

The Free Radicals rock the world, and we have a blast every time we're together. I hope I qualify for the cool sunglasses next time.

My life is richer for knowing Dr. Mehmet Oz. He is simply amazing, and I consider him a close friend.

I love explaining "True Health." My new friends in China were extremely gracious in sharing their time with me. We developed a deep mutual respect.

Being interviewed on TV in China supporting the "Healthy China" initiative.

When you're in the Philippines with tens of thousands of adoring fans, what's left to do except whip out the guitar and give them want they want? We always have a blast when we're in Asia.

This is a time when you don't want to forget your lines—or trip. A beautiful day with my beautiful USANA family on our 25th anniversary.

Playing with Eddie Money was like getting two tickets to paradise. Eddie is a musical force of nature.

Kenny Loggins has an irresistible stage presence. It was a highlight to perform live with him and make great music together.

I'm so fortunate to be in this loving circle of brothers and sisters.

Playing with one of my music heroes, Tommy Shaw. Is this real? Pinch me! Dreams do come true.

One of my lifelong idols, Ringo Starr, is one of the most gracious global celebrities I have ever met.

You might think I was yelling/singing because the microphone was off, but it wasn't. I was over-the-top loving every minute of performing. Sometimes you just have to let it all out. That's when magic happens.

Playing music is so fun for me, I can't help but smile when I sing. Always love what you do and do what you love.

You know I'm having fun when I'm in a full suit in China and playing power chords on my Stratocaster.

away last year. After Dad died, she would often sit in her chair looking at a picture of my dad as a young man. "Oh, Kevin," she would say, "isn't he handsome?" She longed for the day when they could be together again. With all my heart, I believe they have been reunited.

Does your family know how important they are to you? What have you done lately to show them?

We all work hard to achieve success, to arrive at some pinnacle of achievement—to have the perfect house, perfect family, perfect body. In the process, we fill our lives with stuff. Most people have more food, faster cars, fancier clothes, better health, higher incomes, bigger houses, and more conveniences than their ancestors had a hundred years ago. Yet according to the World Database of Happiness,[26] we are not any happier than previous generations. Studies show once we have enough income to comfortably meet basic needs, additional wealth has little impact on our happiness. What we are really searching for is inner peace, and many of us don't know how to find it.

People matter more than things. I partly measure success by how many people's lives are improved as a result of what I do and by the quality of my personal, one-on-one relationships. To develop true inner peace, you must understand what holds real meaning in your life: relationships, making a difference, and living authentically.

THE DOROTHY PRINCIPLE

Nothing is more important than relationships.

Why did Easy Eddie rat out the mob?

Because He Refused To Be Shackled By His Past

I recently got a call from an old friend. We were in a band together thirty years ago, back when we made fifty dollars a night playing in bars and clubs. We were a couple of college kids doing all we could to pay the bills. I remember those days well, getting home at two in the morning then having to get up for early-morning classes.

All these years later, this former band mate called and asked, "Is this the same Kevin Guest who used to play the bass guitar?"

"That's me!"

We laughed and reminisced, and then he got serious. "Do you know who you are?"

"What? What are you talking about?"

"I just saw online that you're on Forbes and you're running a multinational, billion-dollar company. How did you go from being a bass player to being a CEO?"

He wanted to know if I was aware of how extraordinary my story sounded, but his question prompted me to consider something else. Do I know who I am? Do you?

BUTCH O'HARE, WORLD WAR II FIGHTER PILOT

In the late afternoon of February 20, 1942, Butch O'Hare's flight squadron was sent on a mission over the Pacific Ocean. After the squadron was airborne, O'Hare looked at the fuel gauge of his Wildcat F4F and, to his alarm, realized he did not have enough fuel to complete the mission. Reluctantly, he dropped out of formation and headed back to the fleet. As he approached his aircraft carrier, he saw something that made his blood run cold—nine specks in the dark Pacific sky flying in V formation. They were Japanese bombers, nicknamed "Bettys" by the Americans, on course to attack the American fleet.

With the American fighters gone, the fleet was all but defenseless. Unable to reach his squadron, O'Hare realized it was his job as the only fighter left to somehow divert the bombers and keep them from destroying the fleet. The Japanese were about three minutes from dropping their bombs when Butch and his wing man, Duff Dufilho, zoomed in to attack.

Laying aside all thoughts of personal safety, Butch and Duff dove into the formation of Japanese planes, charged their machine guns, and started firing. Butch's four machine guns worked fine, but

Duff's wing-mounted 50-calibers jammed. Butch wove in and out of the now broken formation and fired until his ammunition was spent. Undaunted, he continued his assault, diving at the planes, clipping their wings and tails, hoping to damage the planes enough that they could no longer fly.

Because of O'Hare's and Dufilho's heroic efforts, the exasperated Japanese squadron retreated without dropping their bombs. The tattered Wildcat wobbled back to the carrier, the *USS Lexington*. In O'Hare's daring attempt to protect his fleet, he had destroyed five enemy bombers in less than four minutes.

For his actions, Butch became the Navy's first Ace of WWII and the first Naval aviator to be awarded the Congressional Medal of Honor by President Franklin D. Roosevelt.

A year and a half later, Butch disappeared during aerial combat and was declared "lost at sea." His body was never recovered. In a letter to Butch's wife, Lt. Cmdr. Bob Jackson quoted Rear Adm. Arthur Radford saying of Butch that he "never saw one individual so universally liked."[27]

EASY EDDIE, LAWYER FOR THE MOB

In the 1920s and early 1930s during the heyday of Prohibition, Al Capone practically owned Chicago. He was notorious for racketeering, bootlegged alcohol, gambling rings, and prostitution in the Windy City.

Capone had a smooth and gifted lawyer nicknamed "Easy Eddie," who was a master at keeping Al Capone safe and out of jail. Between 1925 and 1931, Easy Eddie and Capone operated dog tracks in Chicago, Boston, and Miami. The profits were enormous, and both made millions. Eddie's family occupied a fenced-in mansion with live-in help, a swimming pool, and a skating rink. The estate was so large it filled an entire Chicago city block. Eddie lived the high life and gave little thought to the carnage he helped create and sustain.

But Easy Eddie had a soft spot: his son, Edward, whom he loved dearly. Eddie saw to it that Edward had the best of everything— clothes, cars, and a good education. Nothing was withheld from Edward, and price was no object. Despite his involvement with organized crime, Eddie did his best to teach Edward right from wrong. But despite all his wealth and influence, Easy Eddie came to realize he couldn't pass on a good name to his son and couldn't be someone his son looked up to. Eddie wanted Edward to be a better person than he had been, to be able to hold his head high and live a life of honor. After a number of lengthy heart-to-heart talks between father and son, Edward was accepted to the U.S. Naval Academy in Maryland. There, he learned to fly and picked up the nickname "Butch."

Following months of soul-searching, Easy Eddie made perhaps the most difficult decision of his life. Evidence suggests he struggled with his conscience and wanted to right the wrongs he had done. Hoping to clean his tarnished name and reputation, Easy Eddie went to the authorities and told the truth about Al "Scarface" Capone. To secure a conviction, Eddie had to publicly testify against Capone and the mob, fully understanding his testimony would probably cost him his life.

Capone was convicted and sentenced to Alcatraz Penitentiary in 1933. He was released in January 1939. Ten months later, Eddie was murdered while driving home, his car riddled with gunfire. Eddie had given his son Edward the greatest gift he had to offer at the greatest price he could possibly pay.

Edward "Butch" O'Hare was Easy Eddie's son.

In 1947 the publisher of the *Chicago Tribune* proposed that Chicago's new airport be named for Butch O'Hare to honor his heroism during the war. The next week, Eddie's role in ridding Chicago of Al Capone was revealed in *Collier's* magazine. An IRS agent was quoted as saying, "On the inside of the gang, I had one of the best undercover men I have ever known: Eddie O'Hare."

On September 17, 1949, O'Hare Field was dedicated to Edward H. "Butch" O'Hare. The next time you fly into Chicago's O'Hare International Airport, remember Butch O'Hare and his dad, Easy Eddie, the crook who went straight and paid for his choice with his life.

I love this story for a number of reasons. It's a story about the love of a father for his son and a father's longing for his son to be something better than he had been. We don't know exactly what Easy Eddie shared with his son during those heart-to-heart talks, but somewhere along the line, Butch developed character traits like loyalty, courage, and honor. Those traits became foundational pillars for his future decisions. When he saw the enemy planes, he didn't hide or pretend it was someone else's problem. He acted nobly and courageously, saving the fleet and hundreds of lives.

It's also a story of redemption. Easy Eddie decided he could be someone better, and for that, he gave his life.

When my former band mate called me and asked if I knew who I was, he was talking about external things, like titles and roles. I have had numerous titles and roles: entrepreneur, bass player, producer, USANA executive, husband, father, grandfather. Many titles are temporary and have little to do with who I really am. What truly define us are our values, our character, our yearnings, our aspirations, and our goals. It's about understanding our potential and making choices that move us in a positive direction. The better we understand who we are and who we want to be, the more centered and steady our lives become. We become sure and steadfast, unmoved by swirling forces around us.

JEAN VALJEAN: CONVICT, MAYOR, MAN OF FAITH

One of the most beloved characters in all of literature is Jean Valjean, the transformed thief in Victor Hugo's 1862 novel, *Les Misérables*. After nineteen years in prison, Valjean is paroled and issued a yellow passport that identifies him as a former convict and marks him as an outcast. Treated with abhorrence and disdain wherever he goes, Valjean becomes increasingly desperate and bitter. A kindly bishop

 offers Valjean love and forgiveness, freely gives him an expensive gift, and sets him on a new course. Valjean tears up his parole papers and vows to start a new life and become a good man. He assumes a new identity and eventu-

ally becomes a wealthy factory owner and mayor, all while hiding his true identity as a convict and fugitive.

But when the police arrest another man thinking he is Jean Valjean, Valjean has to make a choice. Does he reveal his true identity or let another man take his place in prison? He agonizes over his decision. He owns a large factory that employs many people, and he can do so much good if he is free. But how can he, in good conscience, let an innocent man suffer in prison for him? The old Jean

Valjean would have been glad to escape the clutches of the police and unremorseful in letting another man take his place. But Jean Valjean is a changed man. God had changed him, given him strength when his own courage had failed. Jean Valjean knows who he is, and he refuses to look back. He turns himself in to the police, and the innocent man goes free.

In the agonizing moment of decision, Jean Valjean asks if he is forever a thief, a sinner, a man who cares only about himself, or is he selfless and compassionate, a changed man? A similar question tore at Easy Eddie: "Will I always be a gangster? Do I have any honor left?"

Both men rose above their circumstances and past choices.

ARE THEY ADDICTS FOREVER?

A friend of mine visits a local jail once or twice a week to minister to the inmates. He tells me that most people are in jail because of addictions. A significant number come from homes where illegal drug use and crime are commonplace. These terrible circumstances have been such an integral part of their lives that ending up in jail is almost inevitable. Tragically, because of this, there are many repeat offenders who don't know how to pull themselves out of their patterns of addiction. But there are some inmates who have moments of insight while in jail—experiences that wake them up to the understanding that drug use and criminal behavior is a choice rather than a verdict. These inmates commit themselves to make long-term, positive changes, to break the cycle of addiction, and to live full and productive lives.

These moments of insight and change are unique for each person. Sometimes they only come after someone has hit rock bottom and is in extreme pain and anguish. For others, it happens during quiet moments of reflection after reading or hearing something profound and meaningful. For others, it is a result of a one-on-one relationship, where someone helps them see themselves as masters of their own destiny rather than victims of circumstance. Professional counseling can be immensely helpful. Who a person has been in the past doesn't have to constrain who they can become.

Eric Clapton has a compelling and deeply personal story of his struggle with addiction. Here were his thoughts as he faced leaving yet another treatment facility.

> Then one day as my visit was drawing to an end, a panic hit me. And I realized that in fact, nothing had changed in me and that I was going back out into the world again completely unprotected. The noise in my head was deafening and drinking was in my thoughts all the time. It shocked me to realize that here I was in a treatment center (Hazelden in Minneapolis), a supposedly safe environment, and I was in serious danger. I was absolutely terrified, in complete despair.

> At that moment, almost of their own accord, my legs gave way and I fell to my knees. In the privacy of my room, I begged for help. I had no notion who I thought I was talking to, I just knew that I had come to the end of my tether, I had nothing left to fight with. Then I remembered what I had heard about surrender, something I thought I could never do, my pride just wouldn't allow it, but I knew that on my own I wasn't going to make it, so I asked for help, and, getting down on my knees, I surrendered.

> Within a few days I realized that something had happened for me. An atheist would probably say it was just a change of attitude and to a certain

extent, that's true, but there was much more to it than that. I had found a place to turn to, a place I'd always known was there but never really wanted or needed to believe in.

From that day until this, I have never failed to pray in the morning on my knees, asking for help and at night to express gratitude for my life and most of all, for my sobriety. I choose to kneel because I feel I need to humble myself when I pray, and with my ego, this is the most I can do. If you're asking why I do all this, I will tell you. . . because it works, as simple as that. In all this time I have been sober, I have never once seriously thought of taking a drink or a drug. In some way, in some form, my God was always there, and now I have learned to talk to him.[28]

Hopeful, recovering addicts understand **The Butch O'Hare Principle**: *You have the power to change.*

You can become the person you want to be regardless of your past, your DNA, your circumstances, or other people's expectations. With the help of a higher power, the ability to change is within you.

RINGO STARR GROUPIE HERE

I have always been a Beatles fan. When I was a little kid, my siblings and I would don mop wigs and pretend to be the Beatles. We'd play Beatles records and perform like we were on the Ed Sullivan Show. In my opinion, no other band has had such an impact on the world. The Beatles literally changed music and influenced culture, countries, and millions of fans over several generations. Their impact is still felt today.

A few years ago, I traveled to Liverpool with my friend Tim Brown and saw all of the Beatles' boyhood homes. As a music lover, I felt as if I was walking on sacred ground. I was also fortunate enough to see Paul McCartney perform on stage. After that experience, I set a goal to meet both surviving Beatles, Ringo Starr and Paul McCartney, in person.

I had the opportunity to meet Ringo Starr before one of his concerts in Las Vegas. A few other lucky fans and I were funneled into a room backstage, where Ringo's tour manager gave us a few instructions. "Ringo's going to come in shortly. He's not going to shake hands because he's on tour and he doesn't want to spread germs around. He wants to get in and get out in quick order. I'll go get him now."

As we waited for Ringo to arrive, I watched the others who, like me, were realizing one of their lifelong dreams. Everybody seemed nervous. A few looked as if they were going to pass out. These were all Baby Boomers, people who had grown up listening to the Beatles and watching them on TV. One man kept reminding himself, "Breathe, breathe, breathe." The guy next to me was a professional drummer, and he was about to meet one of his heroes in person. It was a fantastic experience just observing how excited everyone was. We were all about to experience a dream come true.

Ringo was an exceptionally nice person. He laughed and joked as if he had plenty of time to spend with us. He seemed to thoroughly enjoy himself. When I stepped up for a picture, he put his arm around me, chatted for a bit, and showed the peace and love signs that he's famous for. He was gracious and genuine to each person in the room. It was a far different experience than I had expected.

I have met a number of other famous people, many who have been somewhat cold and aloof to the people who adored them. Ringo was different.

Ringo Starr has lived a unique life. He has been an admired international figure since his early twenties. It would have been easy for him to behave like he was superior to everyone else, but when I met him, he treated me and other strangers like old friends. Ringo has spent a lifetime making people happy with his music, but a person like him also has immense power to make people happy just by showing them kindness and regard. Ringo chooses to treat people with respect and warmth. He chooses the kind of person he wants to be. Everyone in the room that day went away feeling good about themselves and loving Ringo even more.

The core values that make up my foundation are faith, family, service, gratitude, and honesty. Those are the things that matter most to me, and I try to live my life by these values. They are manifest in how I treat others and the choices I make. I am committed to living in harmony with these values, particularly when times are tough and I feel pressure to do otherwise.

I believe that knowing you have the capacity to choose and knowing you have a higher power to call upon can have a life-changing impact. Butch O'Hare understood that power. That knowledge drove his decisions, even in times of great danger. He paid the ultimate price for his country, his fellow seamen, and his family. Butch's father knew too. No matter our past, we have the power to change.

THE BUTCH O'HARE PRINCIPLE

You have the power to change.

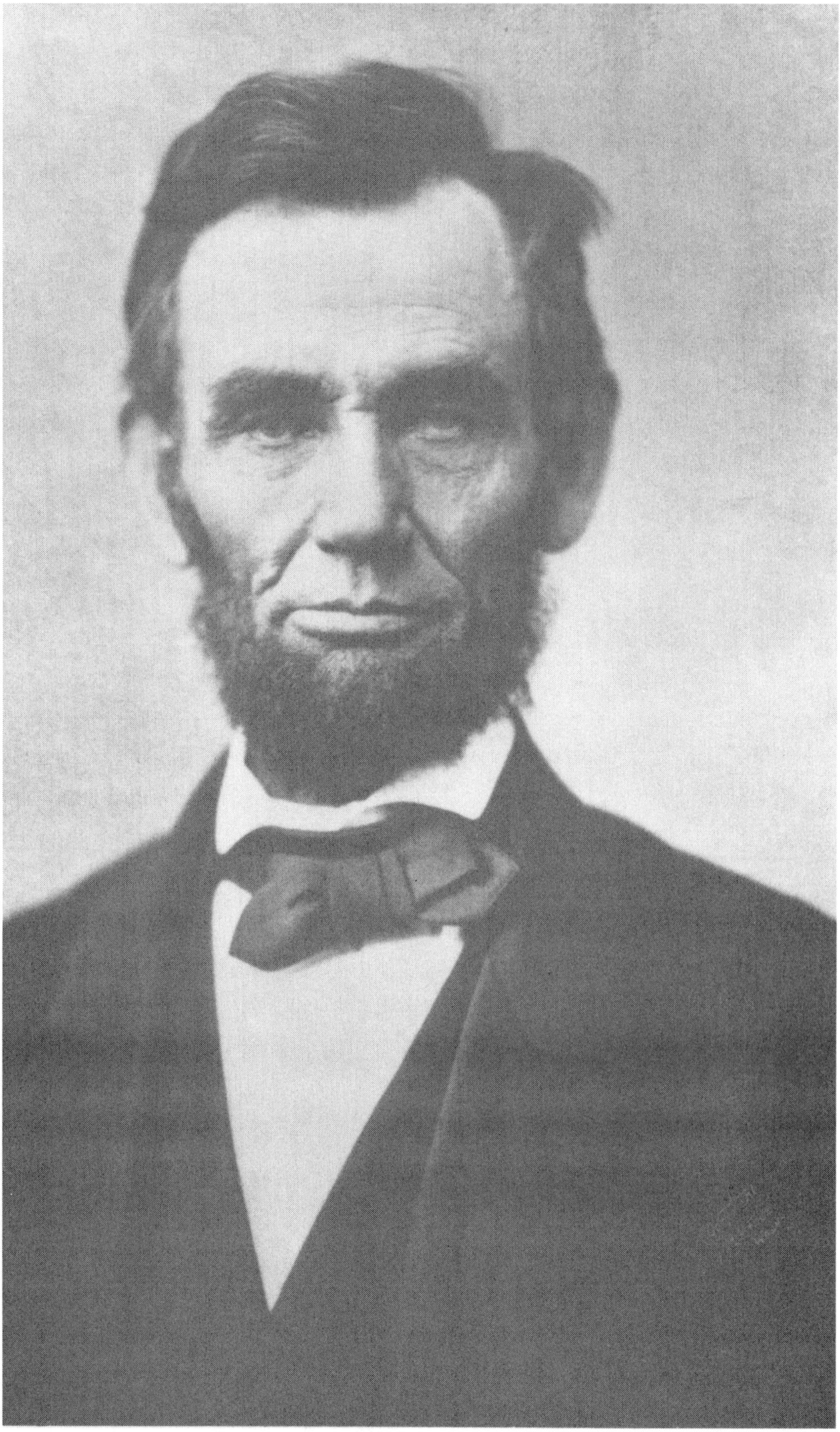

ABRAHAM LINCOLN

*Why did Abraham Lincoln surround himself
with people who disagreed with him?*

Because He Wanted To Learn From Them

Early in my career at USANA, I was in Australia enjoying a quiet dinner after a long day when I got a call from home. My wife, Lori, was crying on the other end of the phone. She had just come from a parent-teacher conference where she learned one of our children was being difficult and disrespectful at school. The teacher said our son and his friends regularly disrupted class and didn't seem to care that their behavior was unacceptable. In fact, the teacher said, our son appeared to enjoy being in trouble. This was not the kind of attitude we had tried to instill in our children.

Lori wanted my advice on how she should handle our son's behavior. Should she implement harsh discipline? Try to persuade him to behave better? Wait until I came home?

My son's behavior surprised me. He was kind and well-mannered at home, not at all the boy his teacher had described. I asked Lori to give me some time to think about it.

Fortunately, I happened to be having dinner that night with Denis Waitley. Along with being one of my dearest friends and confidants, Denis is one of the wisest people I know. Denis is a motivational speaker and writer who has profoundly influenced a whole generation of leaders with his seminars, books, and audio recordings. Denis is the bestselling author of the audio series, *The Psychology of Winning*, and books such as *Seeds of Greatness* and *The Winner's Edge*. I still trust and rely on Denis's judgment and expertise in so many issues we face at USANA.

I explained to Denis about my son and asked if he had any advice for a distraught father half a world away from his family. Denis listened intently and smiled as if he'd heard the same story many times before. It seems there's nothing new under the sun, especially when it comes to raising kids.

After quietly considering his reply, Denis said, "Kevin, I'm not quite sure what you should do, as each child is so different, but there is one thing you must not do. When disciplining your children, don't punish them by taking away something that is tied to their self-esteem or personal worth." Denis explained that in parents' zeal to quickly fix a problem, they often do the very thing that makes the problem worse. They punish the child by taking something away that makes the child feel good about himself. If their daughter loves softball, it is wrong to not allow her to play softball—even if they think it is a fit punishment for bad behavior.

This advice completely changed the way we disciplined our children.

At the time, my son's passion was karate. Had Denis not given me that timely advice, I probably would have withdrawn my son from karate as punishment for his behavior at school. My son loved karate, and he participated in it with a sense of pride because he had worked hard to develop his skills. Taking him out of karate might have made me feel better, but it would have been devastating to my son—a blow that, most likely, would have sent him sliding into worse behavior.

When I finally made it home, Lori and I sat down with our son, expressed our concern for his behavior, and listened as he told us what was going on in his life. He talked about his friends and the pressure to measure up to heavy expectations. I understood. His were some of the same pressures I had faced when I was a boy. Together, we wrote a list of behaviors our son needed to change and made commitments to each other. Things got better. Expressing our concerns and sincerely listening to him were the best things we could have done. Stephen R. Covey's fifth habit is *"Seek first to understand, then to be understood."*[29] Instead of punishing our son, we listened.

I have always appreciated Denis's advice that night in Australia. He had gone further down the path of life and was able to provide me with meaningful counsel. It was up to me to pay attention.

Great leaders always have great mentors. Socrates mentored Plato, who in turn mentored Aristotle. These three intellectual giants changed the course of history. Aristotle tutored Alexander the Great, who by age thirty created one of the largest empires of the ancient world, stretching from Greece to northwestern India. Alexander the Great was undefeated in battle and is widely considered one of history's most successful military commanders.[30] Alexander's success came in part from the collective wisdom of three of the greatest thinkers who have ever lived.

Mentors are people who have learned from their experiences and are willing to share what they know with those who want to learn. *Mentor* means trusted advisor, friend, teacher, and wise person.[31]

The importance of this concept is captured in **The Plato Principle**: *Identify people you admire and learn the valuable lessons they have to teach you.*

Collin Raye is another beloved mentor of mine. People love being around Collin. He is kind and compassionate, always looking for ways to bless people's lives. He lifts and inspires his band members and his audiences, not only with his energetic style, but with his uplifting and thoughtful lyrics. His songs are messages of faith, hope, and love. Few people have reached the pinnacle of their profession like Collin has, and I respect and admire this about him. He has so many lessons to teach. He is respected in the music industry for his talent, energy, and demeanor, both on stage and in his personal life. Collin kept his faith and stayed strong when his granddaughter fought a debilitating disease that eventually took her life. I admire how he and his family coped with that tragedy. His example continues to inspire me.

I have learned from many mentors who probably don't realize they've been teaching me. One person who truly impresses me is Dr. Mehmet Oz. Dr. Oz and I met on the set of his show in New York City while he was at the peak of his popularity on television. Since then, I have been on stage with him at Radio City Music Hall and at several USANA events. Going out to eat with Dr. Oz is an adventure. He is recognized everywhere he goes. Instead of making a quick exit after dinner, Dr. Oz stops at random tables to shake hands and let people take pictures.

At one USANA event, an eager father brought his daughter backstage to meet Dr. Oz. Dr. Oz got down on his knees and spent several minutes with the wide-eyed little girl. He truly treats others with kindness and love.

In private social settings, Dr. Oz loves to talk about health, proper nutrition, and his wife's foundation to educate schoolchildren about healthy eating. Dr. Oz is as kind and personable in private as he appears on TV. He is as personally concerned about the health of our society as he is on his show.

Fame and popularity are fleeting. True integrity is revealed in how people act when the lights and cameras are off. It is possible to have that integrity no matter how famous you are.

The people we associate with have the power to drag us down or inspire us to be better. We need people who lift and inspire us, challenge us, and tell us when we're on the wrong track. I am a better person in so many ways because of the time I have spent with good people like Denis Waitley, Collin Raye, and Dr. Oz. Most especially, my wife Lori continues to bless my life with her goodness.

LINCOLN'S LEGACY

When asked about his model for success, U.S. President Ronald Reagan said, "Surround yourself with great people; delegate authority; get out of the way."[32]

Even though he died almost a hundred years before I was born, Abraham Lincoln, the sixteenth president of the United States, is one of my heroes and mentors. As I've studied his life, I've tried to emulate his dedication to doing the right thing, no matter how gut-wrenching or heartbreaking it may be.

Abraham Lincoln knew how to build relationships. He possessed the unique ability to develop genuine friendships with people who opposed him, even choosing advisors and cabinet members who held contradictory views so he could be exposed to other perspectives and divergent ideas. He rallied the United States Congress, a wildly diverse group of men with wildly diverse opinions, to abolish slavery and end the Civil War.

True mentors not only give us encouragement, they challenge our ideas and flawed thinking. They guide us to deeper understanding and make us question our dearly held paradigms. Abraham Lincoln surrounded himself with those kinds of mentors, and he was a better decision-maker, a better president, and a better man because of it.

When I go to Washington D.C., I always make a point to visit the Lincoln Memorial to reflect on Lincoln's leadership and unfailing courage. The thoughtful inscriptions on the walls of the memorial still inspire me. When I read the Gettysburg Address, I am overwhelmed by Lincoln's wisdom and foresight, his ability to galvanize an entire generation around the cause of truth.

I have tried to follow Abraham Lincoln's example of leadership. I surround myself with people who are smarter and more capable than I am and let them go to work. I welcome tough questions and am not afraid to be contradicted or challenged. The best leaders see the value in opposition.

HEALTH FOR THE ENTIRE WORLD

Dr. Myron Wentz, the founder of USANA and another mentor of mine, is one of the world's leading researchers on cellular health. He started USANA with one objective: to bring the blessings of health to the entire world.

In the late 1980s, Dr. Wentz ran a highly successful virology lab where he studied cells and developed tests for some of the world's most insidious viruses. But Dr. Wentz was also in failing health, and he knew something needed to change in his life. His father had died of heart disease at age 57, and Dr. Wentz did not want to suffer the same fate. He researched several nutritional supplements on the market and realized most of them did no good and others were actually harmful to the body. Dr. Wentz saw no other way to get the supplements he needed than to for-

mulate and manufacture them himself. He didn't start USANA to make money. He started the company because he wanted to help people achieve maximum health.

One passion Dr. Wentz and I have in common is our love of music. Like me, as a young man, he found himself at his own crossroads. He had to decide whether to choose a career in music or pursue science. In college, one of his mentors told him, "You can't do both and excel." Another professor said, "You're so gifted in science and have so much to offer. If you choose science, you will make a difference in the world." Dr. Wentz loved to sing and had a great appreciation for classical symphonic and choral music, so the decision to give up music was agonizing, but he never regretted the path he chose.

Our mutual love of music made Dr. Wentz and me instant friends. There was a specific bass guitar I had always wanted to own, but the guitar company had stopped making them and they were hard to find. Every time I went to a new city, I would stop in the music stores to look for that elusive guitar. A few years ago, Dr. Wentz and I were in New York with Dr. Oz at Radio City Music Hall. That afternoon, I visited an obscure guitar shop and found the guitar I'd been searching for. Of course, I bought it. When I went back to the hotel, Dr. Wentz was sitting in the foyer and asked me where I'd been. I told him the story of the guitar and how thrilled I was to have finally found it. I think Dr. Wentz was almost as excited as I was, and he asked if he could buy the guitar for me. It is still one of my most prized possessions. I played that guitar when I performed with Tommy Shaw of Styx.

Not only is he a good friend, but Dr. Wentz has mentored me in business and life. Music is one of his passions, but even more so are nutrition and good health. Whenever we eat together, he tells me what my meal is doing to my body. He doesn't ask me how much money USANA is making or what the margins are or what our business strategy looks like. He talks about new products and new innovations in health. That's what he's passionate about.

Several years ago, Dr. Wentz was driving his convertible in Europe when he stopped at a stop sign and a man on the side of the road reached into his car and grabbed Dr. Wentz's bags. His passport, his money, his clothes were all stolen. The thing that upset him the most was that he was overseas without his USANA vitamins. He was most concerned about being without his products.

FROM FATHER TO SON

My father was my greatest mentor. When I was at my own crossroads and struggling with the decision to pursue music or business, I sought my father's counsel. Dad and Mom drove all the way to Utah from Montana—about six hundred miles—so Dad and I would have the opportunity to talk face to face. Dad and I spent several hours discussing my future, and I'll admit, I did most of the talking. Dad quoted a scripture, "For what shall it profit a man, if he shall gain the whole world, and lose his own soul?"[33]

My dad knew the scriptures well, and he was never afraid to use them when his children needed guidance. That discussion had a significant impact on my decision.

I want to be clear that I'm not suggesting that professional musicians have sold their souls to the music business. Those I know personally have had great careers without sacrificing their values or their relationships and have made wonderful contributions to the world. But for my situation, this was exactly the advice I needed.

FROM STUDENT TO MENTOR

While I still have many mentors in my life, I also know how important it is to give back by mentoring others.

Once several years ago, I was home alone with the kids. My three-year-old son made a huge mess in the kitchen, and I completely lost my temper. I yelled at him, and he started to cry. To this day, I remember how angry I was.

Immediately after it happened, I felt terrible for how I'd treated my son. I wanted a loving, trusting relationship with him, but I had behaved in a way that pulled us apart. I didn't want my children to fear me or to be afraid to make mistakes. I thought about what I was learning from some of my mentors, and those lessons changed me as a father. One of the most valuable things my father taught me is how to pray. From that bad day on, I vowed to never discipline any of my children without saying a prayer first. Even now, if there is a problem at home or work, I pray before I react. Praying changes my perspective, makes me more humble, and softens my heart. Praying has become a daily, sometimes hourly, habit.

The three-year-old who made such a mess in the kitchen is now a father himself. He wants to build a strong relationship with his own children. He told me that when he was teenager, he never joined in when his friends were doing something they shouldn't have been doing because he loved his parents and didn't want to disappoint us. "Dad," he said, "how can I instill that same feeling in my children?" Because we have worked hard at a relationship of trust and love, I have now become my son's mentor. I told my son I wasn't sure of the answer, but a good place to start is showing our love and patience, day in and day out. The decision I made to check myself with a prayer has made a huge difference in our relationship.

Learn from the people you admire and then pass along your wisdom to those within your sphere of influence. None of us travel this life alone. We need wisdom passed down through generations. You can make a significant difference in someone else's life.

AT THE CROSSROADS
by Sadie Tiller Crawley

He stood at the crossroads all alone, The sunlight in his face;
He had no thought for an evil course, He was set for a manly race.
But the road stretched east and the road stretched west,
And he did not know which road was the best;
So he took the wrong road and it led him down,
And he lost the race and the victor's crown.
He was caught at last in an angry snare
Because no one stood at the crossroads there
To show him the better road.

Another day at the self-same place a boy with high hopes stood;
He, too, was set for a manly race;
he was seeking the things that were good.
And one was there who the roads did know,
And that one showed him the way to go;
So he turned away from the road leading down,
And he won the race and the victor's crown;
He walks today on the highways fair
Because one stood at the crossroads there
To show him a better road.

THE PLATO PRINCIPLE

*Identify people you admire and learn the valuable
lessons they have to teach you.*

Why did Immaculee tell herself she was good at speaking English?

Because Her Survival Depended On It

I n 1994, twenty-two-year-old Immaculee Ilibagiza took a break from her college studies to spend Easter with her family in their small village of Mataba, Rwanda. She never made it back to school.

While Immaculee was on holiday, Rwanda's president was assassinated, and his death ignited a firestorm. Killers from the Hutu tribe declared war on ethnic Tutsis and began a three-month genocide that resulted in the death of nearly a million Rwandans. The slaughter was horrific, with men, women, and children murdered and dead bodies piled along the sides of the roads.

Hutu fighters attacked Immaculee's home and eventually killed her parents and two of her brothers. In the chaos, Immaculee fled to a Hutu pastor's home and begged for protection. The pastor hid Immaculee and seven other Tutsi women in a tiny bathroom where they lived for three months while killings went on daily just outside the pastor's door.

Sometimes Immaculee would hear the killers outside her window calling her name, searching for her. The terror sliced her like a knife. But Immaculee refused to give in to her fear. She spent her days talking to God, thinking uplifting and hopeful thoughts, and planning for her life after her rescue, even though the prospects of rescue looked grim. She survived by keeping hope in her heart and telling herself she was going to be okay. While in that bathroom, Immaculee had a vision of herself working at the United Nations. She asked the pastor to bring her some English books, and while in hiding, she taught herself how to speak English.

After Immaculee was rescued, she made her way to Rwanda's capital where jobs were scarce and jobs at the U.N. were even harder to come by. Undaunted, she went to the U.N. building in Kigali every day for two weeks. She filled out new applications each day and waited all day, every day. She was told each evening to go home because they weren't hiring. After two fruitless weeks, Immaculee started visualizing that she already worked at the U.N. She bought some second-hand clothes, found her long-lost school records, and got her hair styled. She practiced her English, telling herself she could master the language even though it was so poor no one could understand her when she spoke. She drew a replica of a computer keyboard on a piece of cardboard—her cardboard keyboard—and spent hours learning how to type. Not once did she tell herself she couldn't do it, even though everything she had to learn was new and different and difficult. She worked hard and kept positive thoughts in her head until she got the job.

OUR INNER VOICE

We all have an "inner voice," the little voice inside our heads that is constantly talking to us, providing a running monologue for every second we're awake. Psychologists call this mental chatter "self-talk," a combination of our conscious thoughts and our unconscious beliefs. Self-talk can be useful because it helps us process and interpret our life's experiences. Unfortunately, almost all of us are prone to negative self-talk. We tell ourselves things like "I can't do anything right," "I don't have enough time," or "I won't ever succeed at this." And because self-talk is so powerful, we start to believe what we tell ourselves. Negative self-talk can be harmful to our health, our well-being, and our success.

Managing self-talk is a significant personal difficulty for me. Sometimes I'm not even aware I'm in a pattern of negative self-talk until the negativity starts to make me feel unsettled and anxious. I periodically work with a professional therapist who helps me recognize and challenge my negative self-talk.

My therapist has helped me recognize that self-talk is more or less constant. We talk to ourselves when we're awake and in our dreams when we're asleep. Most of the time, we are unaware we are talking to ourselves and that most of our self-talk is negative. As individuals, we tend to be harder on ourselves than anyone else is.

The good news is positive self-talk is even more powerful than negative self-talk, and learning how to channel and elevate the voice in your head can change your life. Our self-talk significantly impacts what we think of ourselves and how we act. With practice, we can consciously choose positive self-talk that makes our lives better.

This is what I call *The Cardboard Keyboard Principle*: *Choose to use positive self-talk.*

DISAPPOINTMENT AT THE GRAND OLE OPRY

I became aware of this mental phenomenon in junior high when my band first started performing. Playing in front of an audience was far more difficult than playing in my parent's basement, where no one was watching. I told myself things like, "You aren't any good. You're going to mess up. You're just a kid. No one is going to take you seriously." Sometimes my self-talk was so negative, I was almost unable to play my music. Days and weeks before our band performed, my anxiety affected my digestion, my ability to study, and every other aspect of my life. It was horrible. As badly as I wanted to perform, the negative thoughts were always there. This internal battle carried over to my adult years.

A few years ago, Collin Raye needed a bass player on very short notice and asked if I was interested in playing with his band at the Grand Ole Opry. The Grand Ole Opry hosts a country music concert every week, and it is the longest running radio broadcast in the U.S. The weekly concert showcases a mixture of famous singers and contemporary chart-toppers performing country, bluegrass, folk,

Americana, and gospel music. The Opry attracts hundreds of thousands of visitors annually and millions of radio and Internet listeners each week. For a country music performer, playing at the Grand Ole Opry is just about as close to heaven as you can get without really being there. It was an opportunity I couldn't pass up.

Two short days later, I was in Nashville with Collin's band about to fulfill one of my lifelong dreams. In addition to the tens of thousands of people tuned in to hear us play that night, there were over four thousand people in the audience watching the live broadcast. It was a huge event.

That's when the negative self-talk hit me right between the eyes. *Who do you think you are? You're a part-time, amateur bass player who doesn't belong on a stage with professional musicians. This is one of the most important performances of Collin's career. Are you going to be the guy who messes it up? You aren't good enough to be here.*

Needless to say, my self-talk made matters significantly worse. Standing backstage waiting for our turn to go on, I became increasingly anxious as I convinced myself these thoughts were true. *What do I think I'm doing? I'm not ready to be on this stage, playing in such an important performance.* My hands started shaking, and my mouth went dry. How was I supposed to play and sing? I couldn't remember the notes to the first song, let alone the others that followed. My stomach hurt, and my confidence plummeted. All I could think was, "You're going to screw this up!"

During the commercial break, the band had two minutes to get ourselves and our equipment into place. I was shaking so badly, my anxiety so thick, I could barely move. To this day, I have hardly any recollection of what took place when we started playing. Terrified of making a mistake, I concentrated intensely on my guitar and my fingering, ignoring everything else going on around me. Somehow, I made it through the performance without messing things up.

Afterward, I was relieved but deeply disappointed. While the members of the band were congratulating each other and relishing the moment, I was numb. That night I had operated on fear rather than awareness, and the joy I could have felt was lost because of my negative self-talk. I had played at the Grand Ole Opry and hadn't appreciated the experience in the least. I realized I had squandered a rare opportunity.

Worry, or fear of the future, is a by-product of negative self-talk. It generates anxiety and inhibits our ability to think clearly. I was well prepared for that night in Nashville. I had rehearsed with the band and by myself dozens of times. My fears were mostly unfounded, but I still gave into them. That night I experienced what Joan Borysenko calls "awfulizing."[34] Awfulizing is looking at the future, considering all of the possibilities, finding the ugliest ones, and following those possibilities all the way to the end.

At the Grand Ole Opry, my awfulizing went something like this: *Because I only had two days' notice to prepare, I will not only play poorly but I will completely ruin the performance. The band will be a failure at the Opry, Collin will never get another invitation to play anywhere, and he'll never invite me to be part of his band again.*

Awfulizing is both irrational and illogical, but for too many of us, it has become a habit. It comes from negative self-talk.

Our bodies react to this negative self-talk as if our fears are real. We produce extra adrenalin, norepinephrine, and cortisol, which cause insomnia, nervousness, and damage to the immune system. Stress is often created by undue worry that comes from mistaken self-talk. Fortunately, how we talk to ourselves is a thinking pattern that can be altered. We don't have to be stuck.

FIXING NEGATIVE SELF-TALK

Thoughts are not reality, not true or false, good or bad. A thought only grows in power when we give it consideration and allow it to affect our actions and feelings. If we don't entertain a thought, it will disappear. Thoughts flow in and out of our minds constantly, but if we don't engage those thoughts, they will cease to exist. In his book, *A New Earth*, Eckhart Tolle counsels, "Rather than being your thoughts and emotions, be the awareness behind them."[35] Pay attention to your thoughts, and let the negative ones flow out of your life like water.

Many random thoughts are negative, and if I accept them as truth, they will affect how I feel and perform. Eckhart Tolle says, "People tend to dwell more on negative things than on good things. So the mind then becomes obsessed with negative things, with judgments, guilt, and anxiety produced by thoughts about the future and so on."[36] Author and teacher Byron Katie explains, "When we believe our thoughts instead of what is really true for us, we experience the kinds of emotional distress that we call suffering. Suffering is a natural alarm, warning us that we're attaching to a thought; when we don't listen, we come to accept this suffering as an inevitable part of life. It's not."[37] At the Grand Ole Opry, I accepted that my negative thoughts were true, and they destroyed my experience.

Most of what we worry about never happens or is beyond our control. Worry hampers creativity, induces anxiety, and destroys peace. It's crucial to develop an attitude of hopeful faith: If I do my part, good things will eventually happen. Faith is positive expectation, and a hopeful attitude replaces fear with faith.

Although we often view problems as burdens, they can be gifts in disguise. Trials and troubles come to everyone, and we all make mistakes—sometimes irreparable ones. Mistakes and problems can be catalysts for learning and progression. If we never had problems, we'd never reach our potential, because humans are prone to accepting what *is* rather than what *could be*.

> *"Good* is the enemy of *great.* And that is one of the key reasons why we have so little that becomes great. We don't have great schools, principally because we have good schools. We don't have great government, principally because we have good government. Few people attain great lives, in large part because it is just so easy to settle for a good life. The vast majority of companies never become great, precisely because the vast majority become quite good—and that is their main problem."[38]

Nature gives us problems to spur us to action, to motivate us to make things better. Recognizing and solving problems moves us toward greatness. Because of my experience in Nashville and the work I have done on my own self-talk, I am better able to control my self-talk and push it in a more constructive direction.

WE CRIED, WE LAUGHED, WE MADE A BUSINESS PLAN

Several years ago, a representative of one of the largest retailers in the U.S. approached my business partner, Shawn McLelland, and me about working with our video production company. The potential project was a series of how-to videos for the retailer to use in specialized kiosks in their stores. The consultant who contacted us asked us to fly to Texas and give a presentation to the top executives who would be gathered there for a meeting.

We prepared an impressive presentation and flew to Texas on our own dime. The consultant who had asked us to present the proposal wasn't able to attend the meeting, so we put him on speaker phone. The room was full of vice presidents and other executives of the company, and Shawn and I knew this would potentially be a huge moneymaker for us. I was only a few minutes into my presentation when the man in charge stopped me and said, "Excuse me, but why are you here?"

I tried to briefly explain our proposal when he stopped me again. "Do you understand how much money is in this room with all these vice presidents? You are completely wasting our time." I stepped away from the podium with my tail between my legs, and Shawn and I got out of there as fast as we could. We had been completely humiliated. I told Shawn that if I had been a drinking man, I would have gotten drunk. Being self-employed, we didn't really have the money to pay for those plane tickets, and we had already counted up the money we were going to make from those videos and kiosks all over the country.

We had bet our future on that proposal, and to be shot down in such an embarrassing manner was absolutely demoralizing. My self-talk could have buried me. Shawn and I could have told ourselves we were failures, that we had no business being in video production. Instead, we determined to use our failure as a stepping-stone for our success.

During our long layover in the Denver airport, we wrote a business plan on the back of about twenty napkins. This laid the groundwork for our highly successful video production company in the years ahead. We had been humiliated, but we didn't let the experience break us. Shawn and I still laugh whenever we talk about that experience. Our belief in ourselves and our positive self-talk made all the difference.

A few years after my first Opry experience, I got a second chance to play at the Grand Ole Opry with Collin Raye. The performance was for a more select audience with Keith Urban, Brooks and Dunn, and other well-known country stars. I determined that instead of being anxious and uptight, I was going to enjoy the experience. I arrived in

Nashville early, got some rest, and took it all in, both as a performer and a fan. I ate the refreshments, lingered backstage, and watched the other artists perform. I met and interacted with some of my country music idols and had one of the best experiences of my life. In part, this second experience was so much better because of what I had learned the first time. When it was our turn to play, I went on stage and kept my eye on the audience. They looked like they were having a great time, and I was determined to do the same. Because of a complete turnabout in my self-talk, I thoroughly enjoyed playing with Collin that night on the Grand Ole Opry stage.

My positive self-talk saw me through.

THE CARDBOARD KEYBOARD PRINCIPLE

Choose to use positive self-talk.

Why did I live in a mouse-infested apartment?

Because I Wanted to Help People

When I was a young teenager, I had a wonderful scoutmaster, Dee Mortensen, who taught me much about service. Dee accepted the invitation be the scout-master because he genuinely cared about the boys in the troop. His regard for us was authentic: he never had to pretend to like us. We knew he cared about us and wanted to help us reach our potential as scouts and as young men. He spent hours with us—week in and week out—for years, taking us on countless campouts in the freezing cold and the blistering heat, leading us on exhausting hikes, teaching a bunch of fire-crazy boys to build campfires, and eating many an unhealthy hotdog with us. He also taught us many lessons about living our values and doing good to others. When I did my Eagle Scout project, Dee supported me the whole way. If I ever needed anything and my dad wasn't around, Dee was someone I knew I could go to for help.

When my mom passed away last year, Dee came to her funeral and gave me one of his big hugs. His presence meant the world to me. He still cared about our family even though it had been over forty years since he was my scoutmaster. Dee Mortensen's unassuming example taught me the importance of not just helping people but of loving those you serve. People can see right through you if you just pretend to care.

PEOPLE DON'T CARE HOW MUCH YOU KNOW UNTIL THEY KNOW HOW MUCH YOU CARE

Shortly after my scouting days, I had a significant opportunity to serve. When I turned nineteen years old, I went to the Netherlands as a missionary for my church. Missionaries for the Church of Jesus Christ of Latter-day Saints leave their homes for two years to preach the gospel wherever they are asked to go. I grew up anticipating I would serve a mission. All of my older brothers had done the same, and I was excited to go when I was old enough.

Just as I was preparing to leave for Europe, some friends from a band I used to play with landed a deal to go on tour and open for ZZ Top, a popular band at the time. My friends were going to be doing something I had dreamed about my entire life. It seemed whenever something important was about to happen to me, like my going on a mission, a distraction would force me to make a decision. The possibility of playing in a band that opened for ZZ Top was an attractive opportunity, but I had committed to serve a mission and kept my focus on that goal.

Before I went to the Netherlands, my entire life had orbited around Kalispell, Montana. My family didn't travel much, and except for a quick trip into Tijuana, Mexico and another to Alberta, Canada, I had never been outside the United States. After a few short weeks of language training and a very long plane ride, I stepped into what seemed like a different world. Windmills dotted the landscape, and the cobblestone streets were charming but bumpy on a bicycle.

Our first apartment had a serious mouse problem, so we put our food in hard containers to keep the mice from eating it. Each evening before bed, we set mouse-traps all over the floor. During the night we heard the traps snapping and counted until we knew all the traps had gone off. Then we would empty the traps and set them all again. No matter how many mice we caught, it seemed there were hundreds to take their place. We had quite a good time catching mice in our apartment, and I'm sure we set some sort of rodent extermination record.

We also didn't have showers in some of the apartments where we lived, so we had fun inventing ways to take a shower. We hooked a hose to the kitchen sink, bought a plastic tub, and covered our kitchen chairs with plastic garbage bags. We put the chairs in a circle around the plastic tub then stepped into the tub and sprayed our-selves. That was our shower.

Then there were the Dutch people themselves. Very few of them spoke English, and they were reserved and wary of strang-ers—especially Americans in white shirts and ties. Even though my missionary companion was from the United States, my first few weeks in Holland were lonely and a little bit disheartening.

I had left a loving family, several close friends, and a comfortable home for a place where people didn't want anything to do with me or what I had to offer. It was a painful shock and a test of perseverance and commitment. I was living on the money my parents and I had saved up for my mission, and sometimes I wondered if I was wasting those funds. My companion and I consistently worked 60 hours a week but went weeks on end without hearing a kind word or finding anybody who wanted to listen to us. We didn't feel like we were doing much good.

As the weeks wore on, I realized I needed to figure out ways to celebrate even the smallest victories. I liked to reward myself when I accomplished something, so I would tell my companion, "At the end of the week, if we've worked a full 60 hours, let's go down to the pastry shop and get a treat." All week long I would work hard, envisioning my reward.

To this day, I make sure there is a reward waiting for me when I reach a goal. It's good to commemorate our victories, whether they're large or small.

It seemed music was always reaching out to me on my mission. Going to rock concerts was against the rules, but there was a stadium right by our apartment in Rotterdam where they held rock concerts almost every weekend. We often rode our bikes past the stadium, and I always paid attention to who was going to be performing. I'm grateful ZZ Top and my buddies never showed up!

Once, as we were returning to our apartment for the night, a big concert was just ending at the stadium. We could see a number of limos parked near the back of the stadium. I suggested to my companion that we stand by the limos to see if we could get a glimpse of whatever band had performed. We were in suits and trench coats, so the guards assumed we were part of the security crew. They told us to wait by the stage door. We were standing by the exit when the concert ended and Elton John came out the door. He greeted us with a big smile and said, "Hello, boys," then got in his limo and rode away.

Another time, the Electric Light Orchestra played at the same stadium. ELO was one of my favorite bands, and I was desperate for a souvenir t-shirt. My companion and I asked the guy working at the gate if he could let us in just long enough to let me buy a shirt. Just as we got inside, the lights dimmed and the concert started. The band started a song I knew, and the crowd was on its feet screaming and yelling. After I bought the t-shirt, my companion and I stood there staring longingly in the direction of the stage. The worker who let us in the stadium walked by and noticed us standing there. He told us we could find a seat and stay as long as we wanted. My companion and I looked at each other and seriously considered staying, but rock concerts were against the rules for missionaries, and we knew we couldn't live with ourselves if we stayed. We reluctantly left the concert and rode our bikes back to the apartment. For someone like me who lived and breathed music, that was the ultimate sacrifice.

LEARNING HOW TO DO HARD

At any time in those two years I could have quit and gone home, but I was committed to serving the people of the Netherlands. My dad served his country faithfully during the war, and all of my older brothers had served and completed their missions. Because of their example, I never once considered coming home early. Quitting was simply not an option. As hard as the work was, my only real decision was if I would be happy or miserable being a missionary.

Scott Peck begins his classic book, *The Road Less Traveled*, with this observation: "Life is difficult. This is a great truth, one of the greatest truths. It is a great truth because once we truly see this truth, we transcend it. Once we truly know that life is difficult—once we truly understand and accept it—then life is no longer difficult. Because once it is accepted, the fact that life is difficult no longer matters."[39] I was sent to the Netherlands, in part, to learn how to love and serve the Dutch people. When I finally came to understand that, everything changed. To use Peck's words, I transcended my pain. Once I chose to be happy and see my mission as a valuable experience, the people seemed nicer and became more interested in my message, and I grew to love them with all my heart.

The great American football coach Knute Rockne once said, "When the going gets tough, the tough get going." Most people haven't developed "toughness" and don't know how. When our lives are hard and problems pile up like autumn leaves, many people quit trying. They quit trying to find solutions, quit trying to endure, quit trying to make a positive difference in the world. But when they quit, they fail to learn the lessons that come from doing hard things. Very few worthwhile things come easily. Even in my business, it is amazing how many people quit before they even get started. Learning how to overcome difficulties, to persist when times are hard, and to be happy in the process are essential to successful living.

Relationships have the power to teach us about service and sacrifice. In fact, we tend to feel more love for those we serve. My mission in the Netherlands was one of the great foundational experiences of my life. It taught me perseverance, sacrifice, and how to love people who didn't love me back. I also learned how to stick it out when things were tough and how to find happiness and friendship in adversity. Love and service are inextricably connected.

CAN YOU HELP? OF COURSE YOU CAN

Each of us, no matter how weak or unexceptional we believe we are, has a great capacity to help others, to make someone's life better. I learned that on my mission. I call this **The Holland Principle: Find opportunities to serve, then act.**

In 2005, Dave Riley, president of ProImage—a sports apparel company—saw a news story about people in the mountain villages of Honduras who walk for miles every day to get semi-clean water. Most of the children in these remote villages don't go to school because they spend their waking hours hauling water for their families. Dave did more than just shake his head at the plight of Honduran children. He decided to do something about it. Dave and his wife, Leona, established Amigos of Honduras, a non-profit foundation, and got to work. A dozen years later, they have raised more than a million dollars and have completed major water projects in over forty villages in Honduras and Guatemala. Close to 20,000 people have easy access to clean drinking water because of Dave and Leona's efforts. Instead of spending their days hauling water, many of the children are now in school. The impact of their project will be felt for generations to come, all because the Rileys decided to help and did what they could.

You don't have to leave town to serve people. There are countless needs, even in areas where money and food are plentiful. How many people just need a friend, someone to talk to or sit with, someone to say hello and care about them? When we give of our time, of ourselves, our lives become richer and more meaningful, and we can make a difference in someone else's life—maybe even *all* the difference. Opportunities to serve aren't hard to find if you pay attention.

When I served as a bishop for the Church of Jesus Christ of Latter-day Saints, a couple in my congregation asked if I would counsel with them. Their marriage was struggling, and they needed guidance. First, the wife came to my office. I explained I could only visit with her for an hour because I had another appointment later. She sat down and began to talk, and the next words out of my mouth were, "The hour is up. I need to go to my next appointment." I literally didn't speak from the beginning of the hour to the end. I simply listened.

Later, the husband thanked me for helping them. "My wife is so much better," he said. And I said, "I think you need to listen more."

Sometimes servant leadership is giving someone a listening ear without judging them. Thomas S. Monson, one of my mentors, said, "Never let a problem to be solved become more important than a person to be loved." Sometimes we get caught in the trap of wanting to fix our spouses, our children, our coworkers instead of just listening to them. Listen more than you talk. To listen intently and to give another person your time and attention is a central skill of great leadership and a key to building enduring relationships.

Too many of us are focused on ourselves and our own personal comfort, and we miss opportunities to help others. Recently while I was in a big city, a frightened, frantic woman approached me on the street. She told me she was running from an abusive husband and asked if I could give her money for a bus ticket to get home to her family. I could tell she wasn't on drugs, and she looked badly beaten up. I don't make a habit of giving money to people on the street, but my inner voice told me this woman truly needed help, so I gave her some cash. I'm glad I helped her, but I wish I would have given her more. I could have easily gone with her to the bus station and purchased her ticket. I regret not doing that for her.

We have many opportunities to help people, whether it's through a religious group, a government program, an independent organization, or on our own when our inner voice prompts us to act. You just have to look and then be willing to do something. When our kids were smaller, we would try to find someone to serve on Christmas Eve. Some years we would serve food at a homeless shelter. Other years we would pick a needy family and buy gifts for the children. There will always be ways to serve.

FEEDING THE WORLD

Some of my most rewarding experiences in service have come from watching Dr. Myron Wentz, the founder of USANA. He's funded children's hospitals in Cambodia, Rwanda, and Uganda and orphanages in Romania and Ukraine. I've traveled with him to many of these places. Some orphanages have rooms full of cribs, and volunteers come every day to hold the babies to give them human contact. One orphanage housed teenagers, and the beds were worn out and deteriorating. On the spot, Dr. Wentz bought hundreds of new beds for the entire facility.

We started the True Health Foundation at USANA to help people. The foundation focuses on areas of the world where people are in desperate need and the program can truly make a difference. So far, the foundation has delivered over twenty-five million meals to hungry families around the world. I've seen the results, and they are amazing. I've been in homes to deliver those meals to families in Africa, Mexico, Central America, and many other places where people have nothing. I've seen the difference our nutritional products, food, and vitamins are making, and for the hungry, the program is life-changing.

I truly believe where much is given, much is required.[40] Those of us with plenty have the highest of obligation to serve and help those who are less fortunate. If you will listen to your inner voice, you will be led to places where you can do the most good. You can make the world a better place and change your own life in the process. As Shakespeare's Portia says so well in *The Merchant of Venice:*

> The quality of mercy is not strained.
> It droppeth as the gentle rain from heaven
> Upon the place beneath. It is twice blest:
> It blesseth him that gives and him that takes.[41]

THE HOLLAND PRINCIPLE
Find opportunies to serve, then act.

Why should you pay attention to your inner voice?

Because God Knows Better Than You Do

On the night of April 14, 1912, the *Californian*, a British transport ship, was 1,500 miles from Boston Harbor, her final destination. At midnight, Second Officer Herb Stone took his post on the bridge. Stone found apprentice seaman Charles Groves glued to a pair of binoculars, staring at a lone steamer on the black horizon. Stone could faintly make out the ship's mast head-light, the red headlight, and the slight glare of white light on the afterdeck. Stone instructed Groves to signal to the steamer using the Californian's Morse lamp. No answer returned.

Cold and aching to retire, Groves asked, "Will that be all, sir?"

Stone nodded, and Groves quickly retreated to his bed.

Second Officer Stone was alone on the bridge. As he glanced idly over the water, a white flash of light caught his eye. Puzzled, he lifted the binoculars and looked in the direction of the lone steamer. Like skyrockets, four more flashes of light exploded in the darkness. Stone quickly notified the ship's captain, Stanley Lord, who had been asleep in his cabin. Lord wearily asked if the flashes appeared to be signals. Stone did not know. The captain ordered further communication attempts to be made using the Morse lamp. The beacon signal was employed a second time, but there was still no answer from the steamer. No one on the Californian was sure of what should be done, so they took no action.

After the captain went back to bed, Second Officer Stone observed three more flashes. But his attention was now on the steamer's fading lights. It appeared the steamer was sailing away.

At 1:40 a.m., Stone saw a final white flash in the blackness of the night sky.

It was not until four hours later that anyone on board the Californian learned the horrible truth.

Although they had multiple warnings, neither Captain Lord, Second Officer Stone, or the young apprentice Charles Groves saw the white flashes in the night sky as cause for alarm. It was a coincidence they had seen them in the first place, because the Californian had reversed engines and anchored as a precautionary measure earlier that night, halted by an immense oceanic ice field. That unscheduled stop in the middle of the sea provided the Californian a front row seat to an unimaginable drama playing out just nine miles away.

The distant steamer had sent those rocket flares as distress signals, and had those on the Californian been more aware, they could have easily rushed to her aid.

The steamer was also sending distress calls by radio. The Californian was well within range to receive those messages, but Cyril Evans, the Californian's radio operator fresh from training school, was also fast asleep in his cabin. From his vantage point on the bridge, Second Officer Stone was unknowingly watching the sinking of the Titanic.

Over fifteen hundred people perished that night because the Californian's radio operator was asleep and missed the distress sig-

nals. The signals were sent multiple times but were never received. On this particular voyage, the Californian had a skeleton crew. There was plenty of room to bring every Titanic passenger aboard. Had the distress calls been answered immediately, there would have been enough time to save nearly every single soul. Instead, the Titanic disaster was one of the greatest maritime tragedies of the twentieth century.

How many times have we received "distress signals" while we've been sleeping, watching from our places of comfort, or simply not paying attention, oblivious to the unfolding tragedy?

Before we can help ourselves or anyone else, we must be paying attention and looking for subtle distress signals. We must be sensitive to things that "don't seem quite right" or situations that make us feel uneasy. This is especially vital for anyone who is in a position of leadership. There are many distress signals that float our way long before the ship sinks. But too many times, we don't notice. We don't understand. We don't pay attention, and we lose the opportunity to save a sinking ship.

Pay attention to signals, promptings, if you will. These promptings are constant and important, but too many times we miss them, and as a result, we miss opportunities to help others in need.

A two-year-old toddler has no understanding of another person's needs. There are three children in the room and three trucks. He thinks he's entitled to all three trucks regardless of who else wants to play with them. After all, we're hard-wired to focus on our own needs before the needs of others. For thousands of years, the survival of the human race depended on a great amount of self-interest.

Fortunately, the toddler's awareness and empathy will grow as he gets older and is taught to recognize and consider that the needs of others are just as important as his own. Compassion and consideration are virtues that are learned by observing others, building connections, and paying attention.

Being aware takes deliberate effort and conscious practice. We are better able to recognize distress signals when we make a point to notice things instead of being absorbed in our own projects, our own lives, or our own smart phones. When we pay attention, we tap into our less obvious senses like intuition, instinct, "gut" feelings, and an ear for God's voice. According to psychologist Carl Jung, intuition is a "perception via the unconscious."[42] It is a feeling of knowing without having evidence or proof. Police officers often claim to know when suspects are carrying a weapon or illicit drugs, even if they can't see them, based on what they feel are clear but invisible danger signals. Your strong feeling may be a sign of something good about to happen or a warning of danger. When we pay attention to and act on those gut feelings—those instincts—we are often led to make a better decision or warned about danger we need to avoid.

MISSING THE DISTRESS SIGNALS

A number of times early in my career, I wasn't paying attention, and I missed blindingly bright distress signals. The results were painful.

During the early days of the video production business, Lori and I lived very much from hand to mouth and were thrilled whenever a paying project showed up. This was back before the Internet and before CDs and DVDs were common. Businesses, schools, and families used video technology for entertainment, training, and instruction, so we were doing everything we could to get into the video business.

My partner and I accepted a project with a small company in California. The client wanted us to produce a children's educational video series. I didn't feel quite right about the project, but I needed the work and the money. We rented some equipment and drove our crew to California for a few days of shooting. We did all of the groundwork and filming. Before we left California, they gave us a check for the whole amount due.

When we got back to Utah, I tried to cash the check, but it bounced. We called the company. They claimed there had been a mistake and told us to put the check through again. It bounced a second time. After that, the company wouldn't take our calls. I found

out later that something had happened to hurt their business and they couldn't pay their obligations. They abandoned the project, stopped communicating, and left us in the dark with a tall pile of bills.

We spent a lot of our own money renting the equipment and taking the production crew to California. That project almost buried our company. All along, I'd experienced an uncanny feeling something wasn't right. Instead of acting on my feeling, I chose to ignore it. It was a painful and valuable lesson.

Back then, I was very trusting and assumed everybody made an effort to deal honestly and fairly with me. I learned the hard way that's not always true. Dishonest people aren't the majority, but they sure seem to get around. Because of that experience, I changed my business practices. From then on, particularly when I was working with someone I didn't know, I always made sure I got paid before I did any of the work.

A few years later, I learned another hard lesson about the foolishness of ignoring my intuition.

We were hired to produce a training video for one of the nation's top plastic surgeons. The purpose of the video was to train doctors and other plastic surgeons. We filmed the video in New Orleans. The plastic surgeon flew in from the East Coast, and we flew in a good-sized crew from Salt Lake. We booked a beautiful suite in a fancy hotel in the French Quarter. The suite alone cost us more than a thousand dollars a day.

I thought everything went well on the day of filming, but once again I had an itchy feeling something wasn't right about the shoot; I just wasn't sure what. We had been paid for our time, the people we were working with were trustworthy, and everything seemed to fall into place, so I let it go.

We went home to begin editing and immediately discovered the problem. The person filming had reviewed some of the shots and forgotten to cue the video back to the end. When he hit RECORD, he recorded over the shots he had previewed. Segments of the recording we had spent so much money and time on were lost. The money we paid for the special camera and the suite was lost. We had incurred extraordinary costs and had nothing to give the client in return. It was a complete disaster.

I had known something wasn't right. I even thought to check the footage while we were in the suite while the doctor was still there. Had I listened to the promptings when they came, it would have saved me thousands of dollars and a lot of heartache. To save the project, we had the doctor do a voiceover, and we combined it with a still image of his face. We salvaged the project, but the client wasn't happy and the finished product was inferior to what it should have been. That catastrophic outcome could have been avoided had I listened to my feelings and paid attention to where they were leading me.

But it is also important to remember that making mistakes is inevitable. None of us is perfect, even the most experienced among us. The pain of mistakes and the work it takes to fix them is where we learn some of life's hardest and most valuable lessons. As humorist Terry Pratchett says, "Wisdom comes from experience, and experience comes from the lack of wisdom."[43] Sometimes, not insisting on payment up front or forgetting to check the footage is the only path to wisdom.

SOMETIMES GOD PRUNES US

Even after graduating from college, my first love was music, but I also knew the video business we were building had tremendous potential. Lori believed in the business too, and we gave it a lot of time and attention. This was during the earliest days of USANA, and my video business was heavily involved in producing content for the company. My band, Midnight Rodeo, was also doing well, and we had a number of bookings that took us all over the Intermountain West. I took video editing machines on the road, edited USANA videos during the day, and performed with the band at night.

Lori and I were able to manage my schedule for a couple of years, but both of my endeavors started doing very well. The band was getting lots of attention, the video production business landed some national clients, and USANA was emerging as a nutritional supplement leader. The problem was no longer cash flow. It was managing the opportunities and the time.

Our band was playing at a popular club in Jackson Hole, Wyoming, where people from all over the world went to relax and enjoy the western atmosphere. One night after a show, a man from Nashville introduced himself and asked why he'd never heard of us. He told us he thought we were a great band and he had some friends in Nashville who could help us get a record deal. We already had a recording contract with an independent record label, but we knew we could do better. We had original music, tremendous talent, and an amazing sound. Of course, we were interested!

The stranger was connected to one of the biggest names in the country music business. His connection had been a producer for some of the most successful musicians in the country, including Johnny Cash, Willie Nelson, Roy Orbison, Glen Campbell, and Anne Murray. He had also done some projects with members of the Rolling Stones. A few days later, we were talking with one of the biggest producers in country music, and shortly thereafter, we went to Nashville for a music showcase for music producers and label representatives. The showcase went very well, and life got complicated.

For years, our band had pursued the recording path, and our hard work looked like it could finally pay off. USANA was also taking off, and our production business was going strong. But I was gone from home a lot, and my absence was starting to take its toll on my family. One morning as I was leaving for a three-week band tour, my young daughter grabbed me by the leg and begged me not to go. As fruitful as my pursuits were becoming, I knew something was wrong. I didn't feel fulfilled or particularly successful, just conflicted and confused. On some deep level I probably didn't fully recognize at the time, my life was at odds with my core values.

Remember what I told you about my core values? God is my first priority. Family is second, and occupation is third. I felt horrible leaving my daughter like that, and her reaction got me thinking seriously about the trajectory of my life. The decisions I faced had lifelong consequences.

After I returned from the band tour, my parents came from Montana for a visit, and I had a long talk with my dad. My dad counseled me to pray about my future and ask God what He wanted me to do with my life, which I did.

A few days later, we took my parents to a large church gathering with thousands of people in attendance, but I felt completely alone with my thoughts. As I sat listening to the speeches, trying to understand what God would have me do, the impression came like a thunderbolt: God wanted me to stop pursuing a career in music. This prompting was completely unexpected and cut me to the very heart. For as long as I could remember, I had wanted one thing out of life: to perform, to entertain, and to enrich people's lives with music, yet God was asking me to give it all up.

I tearfully shared my experience with Lori, and we both agreed I should give up my musical ambitions, forget about Nashville, and quit the band. *And* cut my mullet. We knew it was the right thing to do, and surprisingly, once the prompting came, it wasn't a hard decision. But to many standing on the outside, the decision didn't make sense. We felt like our band was on the cusp of making it big, and I was turning my back on all of it.

Hugh B. Brown tells the story of a farmer who purchased an unkept farm where he found a currant bush that was at least six feet high, all going to wood. The overgrown tree couldn't produce any fruit, so the farmer got his pruning shears and went to work clipping and cutting until there was nothing left of the bush but a little clump of stumps. When the farmer gazed at the whittled down tree, there seemed to be tears coming from the sheered branches and he could almost hear the currant bush weep. "How could you do this to me? I was making such wonderful growth. I was almost as large as the fruit tree and the shade tree, and now you have cut me down. All the other trees in the garden will look upon me with contempt and pity. How could you do it? I thought you were the gardener here. I thought you were my friend."

The farmer looked on the little bush with compassion and replied, "Look, little currant bush, I *am* the gardener here, and I know what I want you to be. If I let you go the way you want to go, you will not be happy. But someday, when you are laden with fruit, you are going to think back and say, 'Thank you, Mr. Gardener, for cutting me down, for loving me enough to hurt me.'"[44]

I have no doubt our band would have done well in Nashville, but the cost to our families and other precious relationships would have been steep. My family wasn't a sacrifice I was willing to make. My core values hadn't changed just because my band started getting noticed.

Even so, giving up music was a bitter pill to swallow. Not only was I deeply disappointed, but some of the band members were very upset with my decision. I don't blame them for feeling I had deserted them. We were on the verge of a very good opportunity. One of my bandmates eventually moved to Nashville and pursued his own successful career.

This brings us to **The Currant Bush Principle:** *Follow your inner voice and divine promptings.*

Listening to that impression and following through on it—no matter how hard it was—changed the course of my life. I'll never know what would have happened had I pursued my music career. After I made my decision, I focused on my video production business, which grew to the point where USANA bought it. I'm now the CEO of a billion-dollar enterprise. As a teenager, I never would have suspected anything could have made me give up a professional music career. Life is full of unexpected turns and crossroads. If we pay attention, we'll always choose the right road.

Even though I chose to focus on business instead of music, my musical dreams have come full circle. As mentioned in previous chapters, I've had more experiences with some of the biggest music celebrities than most musicians in the business. I've filmed Gene Simmons, Ozzy Osbourne, and The Scorpions, played on stage with Tommy Shaw, Kenny Loggins, Belinda Carlisle, Eddie Money, Juice Newton, and hosted Collin Raye at my home many times. These experiences are rare for someone with a career outside of the music industry. It's astounding, really.

The second time I played at the Grand Ole Opry with Collin Raye's band, I found myself backstage with Keith Urban, Kix Brookes, and Ronnie Dunn, and I had the distinct impression God was rewarding me for that choice I had made years earlier. "I am the gardener here," He seemed to say. "I know what I wanted you to be even if you didn't. If I had let you grow the way you wanted, you wouldn't have borne any fruit. But because you followed the path I laid out for you and did your part, this is my gift to you." It was a very emotional moment for me. I was filled with appreciation and peace that I had chosen the harder path those many years ago. In quiet moments, when I think of my precious relationships with my wife, my children, and grandchildren and I consider my career at USANA, I have thanked God for trimming me back when I was a proud, six-foot currant bush. For loving me enough to take away the thing I wanted most in exchange for the things that matter most.

I believe that divine impressions, intuition, and instincts guide our steps and help us avoid unnecessary pain if we're paying attention. But because we are busy, unaware, or inattentive, we miss many of them. They speed past us or bounce right off. Inspiration is the most natural and gifted form of thinking and is available to everyone, if we'll only take the time and do the work to receive it.

THE CURRANT BUSH PRINCIPLE
Follow your inner voice and divine promptings.

Why should we redefine what success means?

Because Mother Teresa Died Without a Penny to Her Name

My dad was never considered a wealthy man, but he always had enough. Being a child of the Depression era, he didn't let anything go to waste. He would have driven his old Ford station wagon until it fell apart if the owner of the lumber mill hadn't insisted on buying him a new car.

Material things weren't all that important to my dad. After he passed away, we went through his possessions and found drawers full of Christmas and birthday gifts, clothes and underwear still in their packages. The clothes my dad wore were still in fine shape, and he couldn't see wearing something new until the old had worn out.

Unlike so many people these days, Dad didn't consider his possessions a sign of his success. Neither did Sister Teresa de Lisieux.

In 1946, while riding a train from Calcutta to Darjeeling, Sister Teresa de Lisieux received a calling from God. "I heard the call to give up all and follow Christ into the slums to serve Him among the poorest of the poor. It was an order. I was to leave the convent and help the poor while living among them."[45] Sister Teresa, now known as Saint Teresa of Calcutta or Mother Teresa, set out to establish a community dedicated to serving the poorest of the poor. Daily she visited families in the slums, nursing the sick, the hungry, and the dying. She started an outdoor school for destitute children and focused on giving dignity to those who suffered many indignities. With the help of volunteers—including former students—and increasing financial donations, she soon expanded her work for "the unwanted, the unloved and the uncared for."[46]

People of all nationalities soon joined her cause, and the international media began to focus attention on her remarkable work. Over the years, other branches of the order were added, and the society was decreed by the Pope to be an International Religious Family.

Despite health problems, Mother Teresa continued her active role as Superior General of the Missionaries of Charity until the last year of her life. When she blessed her successor in 1997, the society had nearly 4,000 sisters, 300 brothers, and more than 100,000 lay volunteers who oversaw 610 houses in 123 countries. Today, foundations on every continent serve as hospices and homes for the destitute and those suffering from HIV/AIDS, tuberculosis, alcoholism, and leprosy. The society's members oversee orphanages, schools, and children and family counseling services. They provide relief work and aid to refugees in times of war and natural disaster.

Mother Teresa passed away in Calcutta on Sept. 5, 1997[47] without a penny to her name. She never got a college degree, never starred in a movie, never made her fortune in the stock market, never worked her way up the corporate ladder. Mother Teresa herself admitted she hadn't done any "great" thing, only small things with great love.

Was Mother Teresa a failure?

The answer to this question is an adamant "no." I'm sure we all bristle at the very suggestion that Mother Teresa didn't "accomplish much," even if she wasn't a success by the world's financial standards. Among her many accomplishments, Mother Teresa discovered the secret to living a life in harmony.

What about me? My band never became famous. I never recorded a single hit record. I gave up on my musical aspirations because of a prompting. Am I a failure? I bristle at that thought too.

> Kingdoms come and go, but they don't last,
> Before we know, the future is the past,
> In spite of what's been lost or what's been gained,
> We are living proof that Love remains.

What, then, is success? Is it a great achievement, like earning a doctoral degree or saving someone's life with open-heart surgery? Is it monetary wealth or reaching a personal goal, like running a marathon or learning to speak another language? The dictionary defines success as "the *accomplishment* of an aim or purpose."[48] Is success only realized by the completion of a goal, something you can show for all your work?

In our fast-paced, in-your-face world of social media and ten-second news cycles, we tend to think about success in terms of fame or fortune. A "successful" person makes more money than we do, or they're more famous or more beautiful. Maybe we think a successful person is one who has written multiple bestsellers, runs a major corporation, stars in a movie, or owns a big house. But is that success or just attainment?

WHAT IS TRUE SUCCESS?

John Wooden, the legendary UCLA basketball coach who had 620 victories and ten national titles, is one of my heroes. He is also the winningest coach in college basketball history. His coaching emphasis was on the process rather than the performance. Wooden said success is "that *peace of mind* attained only through self-satisfaction in knowing you made the effort to do the best of which you're capable..."[49] Success, according to Wooden, is the *feeling* that comes from putting forth one's best effort, even if the objective is never realized. John Wooden understood the concept of a life in harmony.

Arianna Huffington, co-founder of The Huffington Post, believes most people tend to think of success along two metrics—money and power: we see more successful people as having more money and power than less successful people. But Huffington offers a compelling insight: "To live the lives we truly want and deserve, and not just the lives we settle for, we need a Third Metric, a third measure of success that goes beyond the two metrics of money and power, and consists of four pillars: well-being, wisdom, wonder, and giving."[50] Huffington's opinion is that successful people are those who find contentment in their lives, continually learn new things, and do good to others.

Sir Richard Branson, founder of the Virgin Group, said, "In my opinion, true success should be measured by how happy you are."[51]

Warren Buffett, one of the wealthiest people in the world, told Berkshire Hathaway shareholders he measures success "by how many people love me."[52] Of course, it's easy to dismiss money and power as measuring sticks of success when you have more of both than you'll ever need, but is it possible for the rest of us to shift our paradigm so money and power are not our primary measures of how successful we are?

According to researchers at Happify, a group that has made a science out of success and happiness, being happy and enjoying success isn't about money or power. They say success isn't as much about the arrival or the accomplishment of a goal. The *process* toward the goal matters most. Happiness is a combination of 1) how satisfied you are with your life and 2) how good you feel on a day-to-day basis. The good news is, according to research, this attitude of success is an awareness or an understanding that can be improved and enhanced with practice.[53]

In *Lead the Field*, speaker and author Earl Nightingale offers one of my favorite definitions of success. "Success is the *progressive realization* of a worthy goal" or "the pursuit of a worthy ideal."[54] Nightingale believes the journey defines success, rather than the finished product or final accomplishment. "It means that anyone who's on course toward the fulfillment of a goal is successful *now*. Success does not lie in the achievement of a goal, although that's what the world considers success; it lies in the journey toward the goal. That's what Cervantes meant when he wrote, 'The road is better than the inn.'"[55] Success is a process rather than a single event.

I've learned that the conventional definition of success has little to do with what success truly is. In business, there are always challenges and difficulties to unravel. In music, there are always notes to learn, technique to master, and harmony to achieve. In relationships, there are connections to make and service to give. At USANA, for both corporate employees and our independent sales force, we prize the invaluable ability to stay positive in the midst of challenges and to develop a "can-do" attitude, especially when times are tough.

It seems most of our lives are spent on a journey instead of at some final destination. This is why I define success by **The Journey Principle: Success is about the experiences you have, the relationships you build, and the lessons you learn.**

Twenty-two-year-old American skiing icon Mikaela Shiffrin texted this message to herself shortly before a pivotal World Cup race. "You want me to say something that I can't. I don't do guarantees, and I'm not gonna start now...I have no idea how I'm gonna feel on race day. I only know that right now, I'm happy, I'm skiing fast, and I'm having FUN." To Mikaela, success wasn't about winning or losing. It was about the process, and she was having a ball. She won the event, becoming the first person in the world in two decades to win five straight World Cup races. "I can also tell you," she wrote in the same text message, "I'm equipped to handle dang near anything that can possibly come my way."[56]

Nightingale writes, "We're at our best when we're climbing, thinking, planning, working—when we're on the road to something we want to bring about. We are at our very best, and we are happiest, when we are fully engaged in work we enjoy on the journey toward the goal we've established for ourselves."[57]

MY DAD WAS PERFECTLY HAPPY DOING THE WORK

We are born one fine day,
Children of God on our way.
Momma smiles, and Daddy cries,
Miracle before their eyes.
They protect us till we're of age,
Through it all, Love remains.

When I was four years old, my parents bought two building lots on Lake Blaine, a beautiful mountain lake in the foothills of the Rocky Mountain range about ten miles from Kalispell. I spent a lot of time working with my dad and siblings building the cabin, and I did a lot of boating and fishing on the lake. Because Dad worked at the sawmill, he got lumber at a good discount. In his mind, when you could do something yourself, there was no sense hiring someone else to do the work.

Although Dad liked to get in the boat now and then, he was far more interested in putting up a wall or hanging Sheetrock. For years, my dad, brothers and sisters, and I worked on that cabin. When I left home, my dad was still working on it, adding a room here or an addition there. Finishing the cabin might have been the ultimate goal, but he was also perfectly happy doing the work. Working on the cab-

in was his journey, and he enjoyed every minute of it. I also like to think working on the cabin gave him another reason to spend time with his children, teaching us the value of hard work and building relationships that would cement us together. That's why my dad was successful. He took a lesson from every project he worked on, he valued the experiences he gained, and he knew relationships were more important than tasks to be completed.

Once each quarter, I meet with USANA's board to review the previous three months' performance, discuss progress and concerns, and create new goals for the company. These meetings are essential for keeping the company on track and focused on what's most important. We work hard to achieve harmony as a company, and as we consider the past and look to the future, we often have to adjust our plans. During these meetings, I am reminded of Earl Nightingale's definition that success is "the *progressive realization* of a worthy goal." Success is as much about the process of transformation as it is about being transformed.

> Boy moves on, takes a bride,
> She stands faithful by his side.
> Tears and sweat, they build a home,
> And raise a family of their own.
> They share joy, and they share pain,
> Through it all, Love remains.

My dad was a young boy during the Great Depression. He was lucky enough to get a job at the local store making pennies for hours of work. He took the pennies home and gave them to his mom because they needed every little bit to survive. My dad's success wasn't in the paltry pennies he earned, but in the lesson in unselfishness he learned.

Dad was a strict disciplinarian, and none of us kids ever wanted to make him mad. He was raised by a harsh father who hit him with a leather strap whenever he did something wrong. When my dad disciplined me, he always came to me afterward and said, "You do know I love you." I appreciated that. He corrected me, but then he would show love and try to mend the relationship. One of the last things I remember my dad saying was how badly he felt for how strict he had been with his family. It haunted him that he had been so hard on his children.

My dad wasn't perfect, but in the end he was a successful parent. He recognized his weaknesses and was willing to learn from them, willing to ask forgiveness. He owned up to his mistakes and tried to make them right. I can't think of a better definition of success. Or a life in harmony.

GOD ALWAYS KNOWS A BETTER WAY

I have often reflected on that pivotal day when God told me it was time to give up my band, to set my guitar and my dreams aside. My passion for music had governed my life since I had been able to wrap my fingers around a drumstick. Deciding to let it go was an agonizing choice for me, but I don't have a single regret about that decision. There were things I needed that were more important than making it big in Nashville.

I gave up my musical dreams but found so much more. Working and leading at USANA, I've gained a world of rich experiences that have shaped me into the man I am. I've learned that God always knows the better way. He has forgiven me as I've made mistakes, and I've had the privilege of developing close and abiding relationships with some of the finest people in the world, including my family. Because I gave up my musical dreams, my daughter didn't have to grab my leg and beg me to stay with her. I hope I was always there for her and my other children, and I wouldn't trade one day with my grandchildren for a hundred hit records. I believe our family developed profound and genuine relationships in part because I chose to reject the world's definition of success. I chose the journey. And I'm still on it.

A few months before Dad's death, he grew steadily weaker and more frail. I flew to Montana to spend some time with him, knowing he didn't have much time left. While I was there, Dad asked if he could say a prayer. I had heard my dad pray thousands of times, heartfelt and powerful prayers that gave me hope and strengthened my faith.

This particular prayer was short and tender. Dad pleaded with God to be worthy of his family. Other than his relationship with Jesus Christ, Dad's family was the most precious thing in the world to him. I left Montana with a sense I might not see him again in this life.

I am so grateful for the life my dad lived, for the lessons he taught, and the values he instilled in me. His faith runs through me and buoys me up.

My parents gave me a priceless gift: the knowledge that I am a child of God. God loves and cares deeply for all of His children. My parents knew that, and through their example and teachings, I know it too.

> We all live, and we all die,
> But the end is not goodbye.
> The sun comes up, and seasons change,
> Through it all, Love remains.

Ten years ago, I was in Laughlin, Nevada, preparing to play a show with Collin Raye. My brother called to tell me Dad was fading and probably wouldn't live through the night. I considered leaving before the show, but my brother and I figured I wouldn't make it back to Montana before Dad was gone. Lori flew to Nevada to be with me, supporting me as she always has through the years. I decided to go ahead and play with Collin that night, knowing Dad's life was coming to an end. As the band prepared to sing, my brother sent me a text that Dad's body was shutting down. I put down my phone, picked up my guitar, and wept as Collin sang the song I've come to consider a tribute to my dad and to all good people who have finished the journey. My father passed away peacefully several hours later.

My deepest hope is that you will find success, faith, and love on your journey.

LOVE REMAINS
by Tom Douglas & Jim Daddario

We are born one fine day,
Children of God on our way.
Momma smiles, and Daddy cries,
Miracle before their eyes.
They protect us till we're of age,
Through it all, Love remains.

Boy moves on, takes a bride,
She stands faithful by his side.
Tears and sweat, they build a home,
And raise a family of their own.
They share joy, and they share pain,
Through it all, Love remains.

Kingdoms come and go, but they don't last,
Before you know, the future is the past,
In spite of what's been lost or what's been gained,
We are living proof that Love remains.

I don't know, baby, what I'd do,
On this Earth, without you.
We all live, and we all die,
But the end is not goodbye.
The sun comes up, and seasons change,
Through it all, Love remains.

An eternal burning flame.
Hope lives on,
And Love remains.[58]

THE JOURNEY PRINCIPLE

Success is about the experiences you have,
the relationships you build, and the lessons you learn.

All The Right Reasons

By Kevin Guest

(Written for Lori)

We met by chance,
And turned friendship to romance.
There wasn't a care,
Just two people with love to share.
We were young and free,
Captured by destiny.
We fell in love, for all the right reasons.

You said I do,
And said I love you.
We grew closer each day,
Made mistakes along the way.
For better or worse,
Our love has stayed strong, for so long.
We're living life, for all the right reasons.

For all the right reasons,
Our love was found.
For all the right reasons,
You came around.
For all the right reasons,
I found you.
For all the right reasons, I love you.

As we walk through this life,
On your friendship I rely.
We've added more love,
With each child from above.
Our lives have been blessed,
Our troubles have been few, yeah, it's true.
We're living life, for all the right reasons.

All The Right Reasons Principles

1. *The Ben Franklin Principle:* When you commit to living your core values, you change your destiny.

2. *The Piano Principle:* When you really want something, make it happen.

3. *The Turn Up the Volume Principle:* Prepare, then fake it till you make it.

4. *The Leap of Faith Principle:* You act with faith when you take a courageous step into the unknown.

5. *The Hope Diamond Principle:* Good things come to those who are prepared.

6. *The Dorothy Principle:* Nothing is more important than relationships.

7. *The Butch O'Hare Principle:* You have the power to change.

8. *The Plato Principle:* Identify people you admire and learn the valuable lessons they have to teach you.

9. *The Cardboard Keyboard Principle:* Choose to use positive self-talk.

10. *The Holland Principle:* Find opportunities to serve, then act.

11. *The Currant Bush Principle:* Follow your inner voice and divine promptings.

12. *The Journey Principle:* Success is about the experiences you have, the relationships you build, and the lessons you learn.

Acknowledgments

So many people and so many ideas go into writing a book like this. I must thank my extended family: Bobbi Guest, Rebekah Guest Men, Erin Guest Isles, Emily Guest Whitney, Ethan Guest, Oren Reed, Justin Reed, Jeremy Reed, Todd Burlington, Kathleen Lewis, Andrea Holland, Grace Guest, Heather Guest Johnson, Lindsay Guest Hopkins, Audrey Guest Wilde, Daniel Guest, Bob Freiberg, Deanna Freiberg, Joe Freiberg, Sean Freiberg, Jamie Freiberg, Gary Qualls, Sr., Rosemary Qualls, Gary Qualls, Jr., Rhonda Qualls Felt, and Cory Qualls Calvert. And Lori's family: Karen Barber (mom), and siblings Kelly, Wendi, Jolene, Rod, Bret, and Jeff.

I must also thank my musical associates. From the **Free Radicals**: Shawn McLelland, Mike Rytting, Joel Stevenette, Dave Despain, David Mulham, Alan Bergstrom, Tom Hopkins, Michael Dowdle, Jordan Robbins, Rickae Robbins. With **Collin Raye and his associates**: Lowell Larkin, Dan Smagacz, Dave Fowler, Greg Gately, Shaunna Larkin, Klinton O'Donnell, Mel Shore, David Black, Geno LeSage, Sammy Wray, and Randy Harper. From **Alibi**: Dave Shiell, Wes Olson, Von Walden, Doug White, Michelle Conrad, and Steve Goulet. From **Bullet**: Sam Galbraith, Steve Swenson, and Mark Biby. From **Midnight Rodeo**: Joey Maggard, Cordell Baird, Brad Cox, Brian Butts, Jason Perkins, Eric Mangum, Scotty Russell, and Gordon Gates.

I've also been privileged in my business associations over the years. I want to thank Gil Howe, John Foote, Bob Derber, Mel

Miller, and Shawn McLelland from **FMG**. From the **USANA Board of Directors** (past and present): Myron Wentz, Gil Fuller, Robert Anciaux, Jerry McClain, Ron Poelman, Rick Williams, Feng Peng, Fredrick Winssinger, Dave Wentz, Kevin Pinegar, Scott Nixon, and Denis Waitley. **USANA senior management** (past and present): Jim Brown, Dan Macuga, David Mulham, Paul Jones, Jim Bramble, Josh Foukas, Doug Hekking, Robert Sinnott, Brent Neidig, Sherman Ying, Ng Keng Hean, Deborah Woo, Walter Noot, Dallin Larsen, Brett Blake, Peggie Pelosi, Gil Fuller, Bradford Richardson, Roy Truett, Rick Stambaugh, Doug Braun, Tim Wood, Dave Wentz, and Bryan Wentz.

Throughout my life, I have benefited from dear **friends**. They have supported me in tough times, challenged me when I was too close to the edge, laughed with me even when the jokes weren't that funny, and brought out the best in me. They include: Prudence Conley Wentz, Sean and Susie Derber, Joey Alonzo, Lon Anderson, Tim Brown, Bill Bylund, Justin Call, Hunter Carmichael, Leah Cullen, Brian and Amber Curtis, Mark and Vonda Dastrup, Wayne and Kathy Davis, Pat Dunshee, Dennis Eddington, Dean and Erika Ellis, Brett Evans, Melissa Fields, Jean and Luther French, Rob and Kimbria Hardy, Gil Howe, Irene Howell, Rob Hufstetler, Tony Jeary, Brad Jensen, Ken and DeEtte Larsen, Jeff and Laurel Killian, Russ Linnell, Dave Lowitz, Cory Maloy, Ryan McEuan, Pat Melfi, Mitch and Denise Merrifield, Christopher and Mandy Nordfelt, Don O'Cain, Leonard Oftedahl, Alan Osmond, Jeff and Courtney Palmer, Dave Phillips, John Raybould, Mark Robinette, Eric Robinette, Steve Rood, Michael Scott, Gary Simmons, Mark Simmons, Leon and Debbie Taylor, Kelly Thayer, Mark Vallace, Marvin Vandam, Steven Vanderhooven, Dave Welsh, Greg White, and Wayne Zank.

Endnotes

1 https://go.roberts.edu/leadingedge/
   the-great-choices-of-strategic-leaders

2 https://www.deseretnews.com/article/900010669/should-our-nation-
   not-strive-for-morality-and-integrity.html

3 Matthew 7:27

4 Matthew 7:25

5 https://ebooks.adelaide.edu.au/f/franklin/benjamin/autobiography/
   chapter9.html

6 Ibid.

7 Ibid.

8 http://www.hoopskills.com/why-mj-was-mj/

9 https://www.cbsnews.com/news/
   michael-phelps-on-making-olympic-history/

10 Gladwell, Malcolm. *Outliers: The Story of Success* (p. 50). Hachette
    Book Group.

11 Duckworth, Angela. *Grit: The Power of Passion and Perseverance* (Kindle
    Location 3263). Scribner. Kindle Edition.

12 Ibid. Kindle Location 3263

13 https://blog.ted.com/10-examples-of-how-power-posing-can-work-
    to-boost-your-confidence/

14 https://hbr.org/2015/01/
    youre-never-too-experienced-to-fake-it-till-you-learn-it

15 http://www.thekingcenter.org/blog/
    mlk-quote-week-faith-taking-first-step

16 *Good To Great*, by Jim Collins, p. 82-83, HarperCollins Publishing

17 Ibid.

18 *The 7 Habits of Highly Effective People*, by Stephen R. Covey, p. 98–99, Simon and Schuster

19 https://www.entrepreneur.com/article/233890

20 http://www.salaryexpectation.com/component/k2/believe-in-yourself-brad-henry

21 *The 7 Habits of Highly Effective People*, by Stephen R. Covey, p 65–94, Simon and Schuster

22 http://unshakeablebelief.com/2012/04/29/story-cleaning-lady/

23 http://allswagga.com/blog/2010/07/04/20-awesome-quotes-on-character/

24 https://www.winstonchurchill.org/

25 http://jimdaly.focusonthefamily.com/the-most-important-thing-a-father-can-do/

26 http://www.bbc.com/news/magazine-23097143

27 https://www.stlmag.com/The-Butch-OHare-Story/

28 Eric Clapton. *Clapton: The Autobiography* (Broadway Books, 2008), p.

29 *The 7 Habits of Highly Effective People*, by Stephen R. Covey, p.235

30 *Alexander the Great: Lessons from History's Undefeated General*, by Bill Yenne, Palgrave Macmillan. p. 99.

31 http://www.learningservices.emory.edu/mentor_emory/mentorstory.html

32 https://www.goodreads.com/quotes/234584-surround-yourself-with-great-people-delegate-authority-get-out-of

33 Mark 8:36

34 *Minding the Body, Mending the Mind*, by Joan Borysenko, Ph.D., Da Capo Press

35 *A New Earth, Awakening to Your Life's Purpose,* by Eckhart Tolle, Penguin Books

36 *The Power of Now*, by Eckhart Tolle, Namaste Publishing

37 *Loving What Is*, by Byron Katie, Harmony Publishing

38 *Good to Great*, by Jim Collins, HarperBusiness

39 M. Scott Peck, *The Road Less Traveled: A New Psychology of Love, Traditional Values and Spiritual Growth*

40 Luke 12:48

41 William Shakespeare, *The Merchant of Venice, Act 4, Scene 1*

42 https://en.wikipedia.org/wiki/Intuition

43 https://www.goodreads.com/quotes/33157-wisdom-comes-from-
experience-experience-is-often-a-result-of

44 https://speeches.byu.edu/talks/hugh-b-brown_god-gardener/

45 http://www.azquotes.com/author/14530-Mother_Teresa

46 https://www.goodreads.com/
quotes/139677-the-greatest-disease-in-the-west-today-is-not-tb

47 https://www.success.com/article/profiles-in-greatness-mother-teresa

48 https://en.oxforddictionaries.com/definition/success

49 https://www.ted.com/talks/john_wooden_on_
the_difference_between_winning_and_success/
transcript?language=en#t-178087

50 https://www.forbes.com/sites/danschawbel/2014/03/25/
arianna-huffington/#399b44741aa4

51 https://www.linkedin.com/pulse/
my-metric-success-happiness-richard-branson/?trk=mp-reader-card

52 https://jamesaltucher.
com/2011/03/8-unusual-things-i-learned-from-warren-buffett/

53 https://www.happify.com/public/science-of-happiness/

54 Nightingale, Earl. *Lead the Field* Nightingale Conant Corporation.
Kindle Edition.

55 http://www.nightingale.com/articles/success-a-worthy-destination/

56 Time Magazine, Feb. 12, 2018

57 Nightingale, Earl. *Lead the Field*, Nightingale Conant Corporation.
Kindle Edition.

58 *Love Remains*, by Tom Douglas and Jim Daddario